Adopting a Toddler

Adopting a Toddler

What Size Shoes Does She Wear?

Denise Harris Hoppenhauer

iUniverse Star
New York Lincoln Shanghai

Adopting a Toddler
What Size Shoes Does She Wear?

iUniverse Star
an iUniverse, Inc. imprint

iUniverse books may be ordered through booksellers or by contacting:

iUniverse
2021 Pine Lake Road, Suite 100
Lincoln, NE 68512
www.iuniverse.com
1-800-Authors (1-800-288-4677)

Because each adopted child's circumstances are unique, the guidelines offered here might not be appropriate for some children.

ISBN-13: 978-0-595-29724-5 (pbk)
ISBN-13: 978-0-595-75050-4 (ebk)
ISBN-10: 0-595-29724-2 (pbk)
ISBN-10: 0-595-75050-8 (ebk)

Printed in the United States of America

For Callie Lubov,

Who made it all worthwhile.

And
Anastasia,

Who helped lead us to you.

Contents

Foreword

For my husband and me, adoption was the next natural step in our quest for parenthood. Having suffered through four failed attempts at in vitro fertilization, I can only say that there is nothing closer to having a miscarriage than having a negative pregnancy test following in vitro fertilization. Although many people can understand the heartbreaking loss of a child through miscarriage, most cannot begin to understand the pain and suffering associated with a couple's inability to have a biological child.

The physical, mental, and financial stress involved in trying to conceive can leave a couple emotionally spent. It is only after dealing with some of the issues—such as grief, anger, guilt, and frustration—that they can move on and begin to consider adoption.

Many people, including me, began the process planning to adopt an infant or young toddler. In fact, our daughter was never shown to us by our agency. She never would have been referred to us, and had she been, we would have declined to see her video or biographical information. She was too old. We wanted an infant. She also had a cleft lip and palate. We did not want to adopt a child with a medical condition. We had never considered a special-needs adoption—especially one that would require multiple surgeries, speech therapy, and regular medical consultations.

The first time I saw our daughter on the registry, I thought that she was a little boy. We were in the midst of adopting a child and the proceeding had ground to a halt. It had been suggested that we might want to consider the adoption of a boy simultaneously.

I halfheartedly looked at the registry and the cutest little boy caught my attention. He was really adorable except he had a cleft lip. Since we were involved with another child, I did not have any particular sense of urgency about adopting this one. A week later I discovered—*oops!* The child was a girl, not a boy.

"Oh well," I thought "that is the end of that." But I continued to think of her often. Eventually we lost the referral of the child we were trying to adopt. I knew even before it happened that we were supposed to adopt the little girl with the cleft lip.

While it was an easy decision for me because I *knew,* I had to convince others. Her medical evaluation, done by an international adoption specialist, began with the words, "Wow. What a terrible job they did on her lip."

My adoption agent said, "My first thoughts were, why would you want to consider this?" A well-meaning individual wanted to make sure that we were not choosing a special-needs child by default because of what we had been through: the unsuccessful in vitro and losing a referral after months of attachment.

In the usual overkill mode, I did extensive research on cleft palates and lips, and we made an informed decision. We also turned down two referrals of very young infants to adopt our three-and-a-half-year-old. Although adopting a toddler was something we had never considered, we got the most amazing child.

Yes, one tooth is missing, she has a small scar above her mouth, her nose is slightly crooked, and her upper lip needs a little cosmetic work. Although this sounds like a lot, it is hardly noticeable and certainly did not warrant the doctor's comments. Callie is a little blonde beauty. Everywhere we go, people are attracted to her; they are drawn by her happy disposition and her outgoing personality.

We are truly blessed.

Preface

Parenting a Toddler

People choose to adopt toddlers for a variety of reasons. Some people choose to adopt a toddler because of age restrictions that prohibit adopting an infant. Others may begin the process to adopt an infant, but due to unexpected delays or postponements, the child chosen as an infant grows into a toddler.

Still many people purposely decide to adopt a toddler. They may have older children or wish to skip late nights and diaper changes. Some people may choose to adopt a toddler because there is a greater need for parents for these children or because they will fit better into the adults' lifestyle. In our case, the right child just happened to be a toddler, and I *knew* she was the one the minute I saw her.

Whatever the reason for adopting a toddler, these older children present a whole different set of challenges for their new parents—especially for those like my husband and me who had little or no experience with small children. After you have completed the process of finding your child and you decide on a toddler, your work has just begun.

When my husband and I signed the commitment form to adopt our daughter, we thought that the earliest we would be able to travel abroad to complete the adoption and bring her home would be four or five months. We were quite surprised when we were told we might be able to make the trip in two months. That meant two months to pick furniture, clean out the guest room, decorate the nursery, childproof our home, and select a pediatrician. My career as a department store buyer meant that I was used to planning, forecasting, and buying in advance, so the short notice presented a special challenge.

Where to begin? We were first-time parents with little experience with toddlers (or infants for that matter). We didn't even know how to change a diaper. I started by reading baby books, only to realize that most focused on newborns and childbirth. Although there was a lot of invaluable information that I probably would not have been able to find elsewhere, I didn't need information on birth, the baby's first few weeks, getting my body back in shape, or breastfeeding. On the contrary, this information only reminded me that I would never experience the pain and joy of childbirth.

There are many good books on adoption. There are also many good books on toddler child-care. Anyone who has not experienced life with a toddler should consider reading one or more of these books. If you have not read any books on parenting an adopted child or on adopting a toddler, you need to do so. A child adopted as a toddler or older has special needs. It is imperative that you understand and prepare for a child who is most likely developmentally delayed and who may have attachment difficulties, behavioral issues, or other special needs.

Although I have chosen not to focus on the physiological, developmental, and behavioral issues involved here, I have touched on a few. However, I prefer to let an expert explain these aspects of adoption. I highly recommend *Toddler Adoption, The Weaver's Craft* by Mary Hopkins-Best. My adoption agent gave me a copy and I consider it required reading for anyone considering adopting a toddler.

Read it before you adopt and again after your child has been home for six to twelve months. This book can provide great insight into your toddler's behavior. Most likely, during the second reading, you will find information that you can relate to in a new way as well as a few things you missed the first time around. The good news is that children are adaptable and resilient and can flourish and grow in their new environment.

After completing my adoption research, I needed help with preparing our home for the arrival of our daughter and for our trip abroad to adopt her. One question that bothered me for days was, "What size shoes will she wear?" We were able to convert her height and weight from metric to standard, but we didn't have any information on shoe size.

We consulted with both children's apparel and shoe buyers, and we found the answer was simple. There was no way to know what size shoes she needed. We would have to estimate the size based on her age and size and have several different-size pairs on hand.

Unfortunately, I could only find limited information on preparing our home for a toddler. It was much easier to find information on childproofing our home and travel information. Because toddler adoption is usually accompanied by a different set of issues than infant adoption, be creative in your search for age-appropriate information.

What ultimately became this labor of love began as a little notebook in which I recorded items I felt were necessary for a toddler nursery. It expanded into travel necessities, health care, child safety, bath and feeding needs, clothing, toys and other provisions. I began by gleaning information from baby books, adoption books, travel guides, foreign language tapes, and the Internet. Without them, I would have been lost. I hope this book will be as valuable to you as it would have been to me.

Acknowledgments

Had it not been for the families who adopted before us, this book would not have been possible. Many of these families have made outstanding contributions to the field of adoption and give tirelessly of their time and energy. They serve as an inspiration to us all.

A special thank-you goes to my cousin, Tammy Jones, who was able to dedicate her time to help edit my work and offer her suggestions.

To my husband, Michael, who spent many Friday nights having "Daddy and Callie night" so that I could "work." It would have been impossible to complete this book without your love and support. Thank you for your strength in the face of adversity and for never wavering from our dream of building a family.

Chapter 1

What's in a Name?

Naming Your Child

One of the most important things an adoptive parent is asked to do after they decide to adopt a child is to choose a name. This is a very personal decision and helps create an instant bond with your child. No longer a nameless, faceless little person, your new addition now has a name by which he will become known.

Naming your child is often a difficult decision. Many people plan and think about names for their children for a long time; they have already chosen special family names or ones that they like. A key difference in choosing names for a toddler is that he will already have a name that he is known by and responds to.

In most cases, when you receive the referral for your child, you will be given biographical and medical information along with either a first or middle name. Many people struggle with whether to keep or change their child's name; frequently, they only have a few days to make this decision. Some of the factors that must be considered are the age of the child, his cultural ties, and the complexity of his existing name.

Age as a Factor

Your child's age should be one of the greatest factors in deciding whether to keep or change her name. The younger a child is, the easier it will be for her to adjust to a new name, while an older toddler may be more resistant to change. Her name may be the only thing that truly belonged to her, and she may be reluctant to let go. It is who she is: her personal identity.

Deborah McCurdy, adoption supervisor with Beacon Adoption Center in Great Barrington, Massachusetts, advises that "many adoption workers and psychologists feel if your child is age two or over, it is vitally important to call him by the name he is accustomed to, at least until he is ready to make the major change on his own."

Cultural Considerations

A common misconception is that a child's name was chosen by his birth parents and thus deserves special consideration. This is not always the case, especially when children are given up as infants or abandoned. Orphanage workers, adoption professionals, or government officials may have named these children.

Even more perplexing is that the child's given name (the one you receive) may not be the name that the child goes by. He may be called a derivative of the name, a nickname, or another name that someone else may have chosen.

However, cultural considerations help foster a child's heritage. These considerations may be especially important to help maintain the cultural identity of a child who is of a different ethnic heritage than his adoptive parents. Keeping a child's given name can help provide an important link between his birth country and his adopted country. This may not seem important to a child when he is younger, but it most likely will be as he comes to understand adoption and his origin.

Other factors to consider include whether the name is impossible to pronounce correctly, whether the child will be teased about his name, and whether the name is socially acceptable in your community. A Jewish family who adopts a child named Adolph or Dejesus would probably change the child's name. Because words mean different things in different languages, it may be that the child's given name has a completely different meaning, which may necessitate a name change.

Incorporating a Name

That's not to say you can't incorporate her given name with another one. Frequently, families decide to give their child a new first name and keep the given name as a middle name. By keeping a name that identifies your child with her culture, you are providing her with the opportunity to affirm her cultural identity.

Complex names like Alexandrovena, which is a Russian girl's name derived from a father named Alexander, can be easily changed to Alexis or Alexandria. Asian names such as May Kim Lee can be used with another name such as Amber Lee or Louisa May, or altered into Kimberly May. A Mikale or Miguel can become a Michael, or combined with a name the adoptive parents choose and an alternative version of that name to create David Michael.

Another option would be to anglicize the child's given name to a similar name or a translation of the given name. For example, the Russian name Yulia translates to Julia. Masculine and feminine forms of names can be worth considering as well. In Russia, Denise is a male name, the name of a great warrior. The name Denise could easily be changed to Dennis.

Making the Transition

The use of a new name together with a child's given name can help ease the transition from one to the other, even if you have decided not to keep the given name and have changed both names. As your child is adjusting to name changes, it is important to use positive reinforcement to teach your child to use her new name. Never say, "No, your name is _____," if your child uses her given name. Self-image and self-esteem are closely tied to a person's name, and you don't want to create the perception of a good name/bad name.

While we were in Russia, we called our daughter by her Russian name. Once we returned home, we began using her new first name and her Russian name together. The theory is that as your child gets used to being called by her new name, you can start dropping the use of the old name. Many people, including me, use their child's given name as a pet name or nickname.

We chose initially not to keep our daughter's given name but changed it to one that was similar, my grandmother's name, which we used as a middle name. The first picture we have of our daughter reminded me of a picture of my grandmother at that age. Both names started with Lu, and their birthdays were in the same month. We later found out that both my grandmother and our daughter were called Lu.

Callie, who was three and a half at the time, adjusted to her new name quite well—or so we thought. It was only after about six months that I discovered the reason she wouldn't tell anyone her name. It was not because she didn't understand the question, as I had thought. She was unsure of how to answer because she knew what everyone called her and she answered to something different than what her name was. She was afraid to give the wrong answer. It was only after she was encouraged to answer with her given name that she started answering the question.

She then progressed to using both her new and given names. After she started preschool, she began to understand that she had more than one name. Now she uses her not-so-new first name more frequently without adding her given name. Learning about names and name recognition in school helped her put first, middle, and last names in perspective.

Three years later, we still use both names regularly and we added her given name to her legal name when we finalized her adoption. If you find that you want to change your child's name, you can always do it at a later date.

We plan to continue using Callie's Russian name indefinitely. It makes a great nickname because it means "love." Her gymnastics teachers, friends, family, and other Russian-speaking acquaintances use her Russian name as well. We feel that her Russian heritage is very important, and using her given name is an important tie to her roots.

Chapter 2

Baby Showers and Gift Registry

Showers for Adopted Children

There seems to be some confusion about whether it is appropriate to throw a shower for an adopted baby or toddler. Let me set the record straight: It is a perfectly acceptable practice to throw a shower for an adopted child. While pregnancy is an exciting time for a mother-to-be, it is equally exciting or perhaps even more so for adoptive parents, because they have undergone sometimes years of watching their friends and coworkers announce their pregnancies and suffering through or avoiding multiple baby showers. When it's finally their turn, no one deserves it more.

The hardest part of planning a shower for adoptive parents is trying to choose the date. In cases of a domestic private, open, or independent adoption for infants, the adoptive parents would know when their baby is due. But in adoptions through the Department of Social Services, adoptive parents may just get a call that there is a child waiting for them. In the case of international adoption, there can be numerous unexpected delays. There is also the possibility that an adoption could fall through before or even after the shower has been given. Even considering these unique situations, there are many creative ways to throw a shower for adoptive parents.

Types of Showers

A Secret Shower: This shower is perfect for people who have been on a waiting list for a child and get an unexpected call that a child is available for them at once. Usually these people have done little or no preparation and need everything. A friend told me that this happened to a couple at her church. The women at her church bought much-needed baby items and wrapped them without cards and names. The items were delivered to the couple's home from the church, leaving them free to write one thank-you note rather than individual notes. This was a thoughtful option for a couple who had their hands full rearranging their household and adjusting to a new addition with such short notice.

A One-Month or Coming-Out Shower: This shower is thrown a few weeks or a month after the child arrives. It's a great way to introduce friends to the new addition, and it gives both parents and child an adjustment period. This shower is ideal for unexpected arrivals as well as for toddlers and older children. After a few weeks, there is a good chance that the parents will have most of the essentials. Shopping is easy because guests know the sex of the child. Clothing is a good idea, especially if the child is a toddler or older. For internationally adopted children, size information is unavailable, and weight and height information may not be accurate—especially if there has been a delay in the adoption process. For infants, I like to buy clothes they can grow into. Photo albums, memory books and boxes, and picture frames become cherished keepsakes. Books are a great gift; and I also like to give educational videos, savings bonds, and, of course, toys.

The Traditional Shower: Although this type of shower can actually be the most helpful in preparing for a new child, it can also be the trickiest to plan, especially if it is an international adoption. For example, we signed our commitment to adopt first and then did all of the other paperwork, including the Home Study and Bureau of Citizenship and Immigration Services (BCIS) approval. We were told that we would be able to travel to get our child approximately two weeks after receiving our INS approval. As a result, our friends and coworkers planned tentative showers and waited until the last minute to send out invitations. When BCIS indicated that we would be receiving our approval within the next week, shower invitations were mailed.

Gift Registry

Gift registries for adopted children are an acceptable practice; in fact, it is easier for friends and family to make selections because toddlers have different needs and many traditional baby gifts are not appropriate. Appropriate gifts also depend on the child's developmental level, which can be directly associated with their length of time in the orphanage or another less-than-desirable situation. I don't recommend buying clothing because it is difficult to figure out the sizes until the parents actually see their child.

Retailers Don't Recognize Adoptive Families

Warning, warning! Be prepared for registry questionnaires that are not necessarily appropriate for an adopted child. I felt as though I had to constantly explain myself. It is also not uncommon to get strange looks from people who can't understand why you are doing a baby registry, talking about the shower you just had, or exchanging gifts when you don't look even slightly pregnant. One salesperson actually asked me if my purchase was for my first grandchild, which would be impossible unless I had had a child in my teens. Trust me, I don't look that old!

I could not find any registry programs for adopted children, although there are many for parents of newborns and multiples. In fact, a representative from the largest toy and baby store on the East Coast sent me a handwritten note congratulating me on my pregnancy. They followed up with a customer service survey form. I informed them that while I appreciated a handwritten note, I was not pregnant—and the registrar knew that when I registered.

I also could not redeem their certificate for a diaper bag, since I would not be having a newborn and suggested they consider a registry program appropriate for adoptive parents. Though my friends spent hundreds of dollars in this store, the store representatives didn't bother to send me a reply. That was a valuable lesson. Now I save all correspondence I send to companies suggesting services for adopting parents and their children.

Request Services

As an adoptive parent with almost twenty years' retail experience, I urge everyone to contact the retailers whose stores they frequent and the manufacturers whose products they buy and request programs and services for adopted children. Until enough interest is expressed to show a growing market of adoptive parents, we will continue to be either excluded from or ineligible for many programs for new families.

Retailers are always looking for niche markets and trying to increase their market share. Recently, several companies have started to recognize adoptive families and include them in their advertising. Now is the time for adoptive families to flex their collective muscle. As in *Horton Hears a Who*, we need to keep saying, "We're here, we're here!"

Manufacturers use consumer requests in considering product/program development. As the number of adoptive families continues to increase, so does our importance as a consumer market. Your voice can make a difference. I say, ask, ask often, and ask loudly.

I send the following request to companies that I feel are missing programs that suit the needs of adoptive parents:

While you have programs for newborns and multiples, I noticed that you do not currently have any programs for adoptive parents/children. As a consumer who regularly uses your products, I would urge you to consider a program for adoptive families. Most internationally adopted babies are 6 to 24 months of age, not newborns. Adoptive families miss out on many special programs, promotional items, giveaways, etc., because there are no programs for adopted children—only infants, newborns, and multiples.

I urge you to use this request as often as you see fit. Adopted babies or toddlers are just as special as biological children are. When enough people request these services, companies will realize the validity of our request.

Return/Exchange Policies

Know the return/exchange policy of the stores where you shop and register. Is there a time limit for exchanges? Keeping sales receipts will help make returns and exchanges easier to process.

Because we believed we would be traveling to get our daughter within a month of our baby showers, we opened our presents and put her things where they belonged. However, unexpected delays within the foreign government kept us from traveling as expected. As a result, Callie had outgrown many items, which could not be returned because we had opened them. Don't open any items that could possibly be outgrown or left unused until after you get your court date or you return home with your child. Stores should let you exchange basic merchandise that is part of their everyday assortment.

Usually, fashion items and clothing can only be returned/exchanged during the current selling season. If the item gets marked down, you will only be credited for the markdown price without the receipt. Don't hold onto an item that you suspect you will not be able to use. It's better to get a merchandise credit than to be stuck with an item you cannot use. Your friends will understand if your child was not able to wear the outfit that they bought. If you're afraid you'll hurt someone's feelings, try to exchange the clothing for a larger size.

When returning and exchanging merchandise, sympathetic salespeople can be your greatest allies. Don't be afraid to tell people you are adopting a child and you're not sure of her size, so you need a bigger size or a merchandise credit, or that your travel plans have been postponed, so now you need to return or exchange things your child has outgrown. One store manager was gracious enough to let me exchange a coat several months after the time limit had expired. Of course, it didn't hurt that the new coat I bought was two sizes larger and three times as expensive as the one I returned. However, if I had been afraid to ask or had not explained our situation, I would have had to buy a new coat as well as keep one that was too small.

Chapter 3

While You Are Waiting

While you are waiting to complete the adoption of your child, there are many things that you can do to occupy your time. Staying active will—at least in theory—help the time pass more quickly.

Actually this is probably an adoption myth. We all know once we accept a referral we can't wait to get our hands on the little fellow and no amount of busywork can truly take away that longing. However, you should make the most out of the time you have now; you will not have that luxury when your new addition arrives.

Meet Other Adoptive Families

Meeting and talking with other adoptive families helps creates a connection with someone who has been or is experiencing the same things you are. Adoptive families are unique, and often nonadoptive friends and families have a hard time comprehending what you are going through.

For international adoptions, it can be beneficial to network with families who have recently been to the country, region, city, or even the same orphanage. Of course, there is no such thing as a sure thing, but you can get a general idea about how long your trip will be, if the judge will waive the waiting period, what to expect at the court procedures.

It is also a good idea to find out what your options are concerning accommodations, restaurants, places to see, and places to shop. We spoke to several people who had recently traveled to our daughter's region, and having this information was a lifesaver.

When we went to Russia, we were told that we had been booked into new accommodations, a renovated health spa surrounded by woods. I had requested a popular hotel, but arrangements had already been made. The hotel was terrible. It was not really a hotel; there were no other guests, only the people who worked there. Apparently, the owner of the large multi-story building rented it out by the room. It was very isolated, even though it was in the middle of the city. We probably would not have been able to leave the grounds or even our room, and I did not feel safe. It reminded me more of an abandoned building than a renovated one.

After we finished looking around, we asked to change accommodations and were able to give the names of the hotels we wanted. Our interpreter was uncomfortable translating this request. Later, however, she told me she did not know why they had put us at the old spa in the first place because all the businesspeople she dealt with usually stayed at the hotel I had requested. Our facilitators did not have a problem moving us, and it was done within an hour. This did not in any way affect our relationship with our facilitators, with whom we still have regular contact. In fact, they were impressed that I knew so much about their city, hotels, and restaurants.

Parenting Classes

Take a parenting class. First-time parents may be understandably nervous or have no idea how to care for a toddler. Unfortunately, unless you live in a larger metropolitan area, the only child-care classes available may be for expectant pregnant parents and many expectant adoptive parents may not feel comfortable in that environment. The majority of the information covered in these classes involves childbirth, hospital stays, and procedures. We certainly had no desire or plans to subject ourselves to one of these classes, but we bit the bullet prior to an impending adoption of a newborn. (If you think you don't know how to take care of a toddler, just try to imagine what is required for an infant!) I was relieved when we arrived to find that we were not the only adoptive couple there.

Another option is to take a child-care course for child-care providers. Check with your local Red Cross or technical colleges to see what type of classes they offer. In addition to child-care classes, you should take an infant or child CPR class.

One of the hospitals in our area has started offering classes for adoptive parents. They are for newborn/infant care and are by special request. These classes were not available six months ago. If your adoption is taking longer than anticipated, check back with your area agencies to find out what is currently available.

If the classes you need are not available, try requesting that they add the type of program you need. Our hospital was very open to the possibility of providing toddler care classes. I also suggested that they advertise their adoption classes with local adoption agencies, attorneys, pediatricians, and other special-interest groups.

Preschool Programs

Check out your daycare and preschool options. Your needs will vary greatly depending on when you will be returning to work. Sign up for the waiting list if necessary. If an adoption will be completed shortly, you may have to begin making payments to ensure your child's space is held.

Our daughter was three-and-a-half years old at the time of her adoption. Her developmental level was more like that of a two-and-a-half- to three-year-old. We decided not to rush her into a preschool program. We formed an adoption playgroup. We had also joined a Mommies Day Out program for several months but found that it did not have enough structure. Check out similar programs and make sure that it is a structured learning environment. It may be counterproductive for one of your child's first classroom experiences to be one of chaos, including little supervised play, inconsistent caretakers, and little educational value.

We decided to hold Callie back a year in school. When she was four, she began three-year-old preschool. In that particular program, I could have changed her to the four-year-old class if necessary.

Daycare and preschool programs should have an open-door policy and encourage parent participation. I inquired about observing one 4K class I had considered for Callie and was told no because it was considered disruptive to the classroom. The teacher went on to tell me that the policy was to protect the children's privacy and that they had parent open house once a year. I don't believe a four-year-old's "right to privacy" is more important than a parent's right to observe a classroom when trying to choose a safe and appropriate school program. We did not apply to that program.

Learn the Language

If you are adopting internationally, learn some of the basics in your child's native language. (My husband learned two: *peeva*, which means "beer," and *spasiba*, "thank you.") Your host will appreciate the effort, and it may be comforting to your child if you can say a few words or phrases that he can understand.

When we decided to adopt from Russia a second time, I decided to improve my Russian language skills and listened to language-learning tapes in the car while waiting to pick Callie up from preschool. Other ways to become familiar with the new language are listening to music or renting a foreign-language film.

Most bookstores have an assortment of foreign-language materials. Depending on what is available, you may have to special-order them. Available programs include *Berlitz Passport to 31 Languages, Berlitz Phrase Book and Dictionary* (these are great to carry in a handbag or pocket), *Living Languages In-Flight Programs,* and Teresa Kellehers *Adopting from Russia, a Language and Parenting Guide.*

Rest and Relaxation

A stressed-out Mommy can make for a stressed-out family. It is important to take care of yourself while you are preparing for your adoption. Infertility and grief alone can cause crisis-level stress. Add waiting, delays, or postponements, and some days you might have to make yourself get out of bed. Sometimes it's good to play hooky and stay in bed all day.

If you look good, you'll feel good. Have your nails done; get a pedicure or a massage. Have a makeover, try a new haircut, or color your hair. Always wanted to be a blonde? Now's a great time to go for it!

Try wearing bright colors instead of muted or dark shades. Play dress-up; try on clothing in the latest styles or colors even if you think it's not for you—you might be surprised. Update your wardrobe and get rid of all those baggy, pregnant-wannabe clothes. Have "glamour photos" taken, or make your own calendar. Some other things that can help are:

- Cook a favorite time-consuming meal instead of takeout
- Don't overextend yourself, especially during the holidays
- Go to quiet, dimly lit restaurants instead of loud, crowded bars and restaurants
- Have quiet, intimate evenings with a few friends instead of large parties
- If you host an annual event, see if a friend would be willing to host this year
- Listen to jazz or classical music

•Spend a day at a spa
•Take a relaxing bubble bath
•Take a small vacation
•Unplug the phone (This is a hard one if you are waiting for "the call.")
•Use candles at dinner
•Visit a favorite childhood spot
•Visit out-of-town friends or family

Diet and Exercise

Now is probably not the best time to start a diet. Caffeine, chocolate, and doughnuts are good antidotes to stress. My medicine of choice is sugar cookies with frosting and birthday cake.

If you do not have a daily exercise routine, now is a good time to start. If you travel to adopt your child, you may do a large amount of walking or be on your feet longer than usual. Carrying around or picking up a toddler without having the opportunity to become accustomed to it can result in backache or injury. Walking twenty to twenty minutes a day can help increase your stamina and is good for your back.

If you skip the sodas, chocolate or doughnuts, you may even lose a few pounds. This could be an added bonus, especially if you are carrying around twenty-five or thirty pounds of IVF/fertility-drug-induced "side effects."

Read

Now is the time to study up. Read parenting, toddler, and adoption books. Reading is also a great way to take your mind off your adoption. Read for leisure, study up on a hobby or sport, read the biography of someone you admire, or read trashy romance novels! Reread an old favorite, finish the one you already started but haven't had time to finish, or read something you've always wanted to read.

Paperwork

You thought you were through with the paperwork. Now is a good time to gather the documents needed for your child's Social Security card. Find out what is needed to obtain your child's passport, the requirements for re-adoption, state subsidies or grants, or tax information. Complete any paperwork that you can in advance, including insurance and medical forms.

Keeping Busy

Nothing makes me feel better than shopping. Shop for your new arrival, and make the purchases necessary to begin life as a family. Complete a gift registry, purchase gifts and donations for your trip, or do your Christmas shopping early. The following will also help keep you busy: You didn't know you had so much work to do did you?

- Begin a lifebook
- Childproof your house
- Clean the house
- Complete your nursery
- Finish a project
- Get immunizations
- Have the carpets cleaned
- Have the house painted
- Keep a diary
- Learn about children's toys
- Learn to change a diaper
- Make a list of questions to ask your child's caregiver
- Pick adoption announcements
- Plan the christening
- Plant flowers, bulbs, or gardens
- Renovate/redecorate your bathroom

•Research children's services
•Select a pediatrician
•Select godparents
•Stock your pantry
•Write your will

Chapter 4

The Toddler Wardrobe

Shopping for Your New Arrival

The first thing I did after we accepted the referral of our daughter was buy a pair of toddler bunny slippers. (In my defense, it was May and they were on sale.) Three dresses, a short set, and a package of socks followed the slippers. I was afraid if I didn't buy ahead that there would be nothing to choose from when it was time to travel. With a little help from my mother, by the time we were supposed to travel, I had a complete summer wardrobe for a thirteen-month-old child.

After several months of travel postponements, I had acquired a complete winter wardrobe, including a wool coat, for our now sixteen-month-old girl. While we began the adoption process to adopt a thirteen-month-old child, we actually adopted a three-year-old. Over a year had passed from the time we started the adoption process until the time we adopted our daughter. We had clothes in size 18 months to 4T.

I found that planning and updating a wardrobe for our daughter was on some levels therapeutic. (I love being able to justify shopping.) At the time of our adoption, our nursery had been completed for about a year and shopping for clothing was one way I could continue to plan for the arrival of our child. While there are some things she had outgrown and could not use, it was still cheaper than regular therapy would have been!

What Size Clothing?

Generally speaking, if you are adopting a toddler in the United Sates, you will probably be given accurate clothing and shoe sizes. Those who adopt internationally may not have that luxury. The most they can hope for is that sympathetic orphanage directors, facilitators, or adoption agencies provide the most up-to-date, accurate information available.

When we began procedures for adopting Callie, we requested current size and weight information. Her records had not been updated in almost a year. Because there was such a difference in size, we believed one or both of the size reports were inaccurate. We had also requested an updated video of our child, which was very difficult to obtain, so we did not even consider requesting size information a second time.

Our daughter's "updated" measurements, taken six months before her adoption, were still five pounds light. She was so small that the doctor at the U.S. embassy weighed her twice because he thought something was wrong with the scales. When we factored in how much we thought she should have grown, we ended up taking size 3T and 4T clothing. Callie was really a 2T, but most of the outfits fit by the following spring. The first year home, Callie gained six pounds and grew six inches. One advantage of the two-trip system that many Eastern European countries and Russia have implemented is that you can measure your child in person. You can purchase clothing that is the correct size when you return home and are waiting for your court date.

Some families were given correct measurements including height, weight, leg length, foot length, and arm length. This is rare and I had no clue where to begin to figure out her shoe size.

What Size Shoes?

Most of the shoes Callie wore during our orphanage visits did not fit. Her little feet stuck out of the sides of her sandals. They were also so well worn they would not have been sold at a resale shop.

One question that perplexed me for days was "What size shoes will she wear?" Although our figures were inaccurate, we were able to convert her height and weight from metric to standard, but we had no way to get any information about shoe size. After consulting with both children's apparel and shoe buyers, the answer was quite simple: There is no way to know what size shoes you will need. You will have to estimate based on age and size and have several different-size pairs on hand.

I recommend buying inexpensive white or black shoes that can be returned or left at the orphanage if they don't fit. Leather or leather-look shoes can be cleaned more easily and will last longer than canvas shoes. They will also be greatly appreciated and will help lighten your load for the return trip home—or in my case, make room for more souvenirs.

Whoever invented shoes with Velcro closures was a genius. Kids can put them on or take them off by themselves. I really liked this aspect of the shoes that I left at the orphanage. I had seen the children slip buckled shoes on and off.

If you are able to visit your child prior to the adoption, you may be able to measure his feet to see what size shoes he will need. To do this, trace his foot on a piece of paper. Take this measurement with or without socks, depending on if they will be worn with the shoes. Measure the longest part of the foot from the longest toe to the heel. Use the following infant and toddler size chart for conversion.

Shoe Size	Foot Length in Inches
1	3 8/16
2	3 7/8
3	4 3/16
4	4½
5	4 13/16
6	5 1/8
7	5½
8	5¾

Clothing Sizes and Size Charts

Between the time I managed a children's clothing store and the time we started the adoption process, the sizes for children's clothing were changed. Now in addition to the standard sizes of 18 months, 24 months, 2T, and so on, we now have sizes like infant, XX-small, and 3 years. Somewhere along the way, the new "in" stores decided to create their own sizes. Thankfully the manufacturers that have been in the business for years did not change standard industry sizing.

Basically this inconsistency in children's clothing sizes requires you to know multiple size charts depending on the store. In essence, if you shop at a department store or a discount store, your child will wear one size (with the exception of a few designer brands that may be available), but if you shop at Baby Gap or Old Navy, for example, your child will wear multiple sizes.

I stumbled on this phenomenon quite by accident when a friend, whose child was much younger than the one we were adopting, asked me what size our child was and then replied that her son wore the same size. I knew that, with the age difference, this could not possibly be true. I can't imagine the confusion that this has caused gift-givers all over the country. I had firsthand experience with this problem when I was given the size for my cousin's daughter, 24 months. Was this 24 months the size that should fit a 25- to 28-pound child or the size that should fit a two-year-old? Adding to the confusion was the fact that she was only eighteen months old.

The following size charts are two examples of how children's clothing sizes may vary:

Size	Weight (pounds)	Height (inches)
0–5 months	7–13	Up to 24
6–9 months	14–19	24–28
12 months	20–22	28–30
18 months	23–25	31–32
24 months	26–28	33–35
2T	26–28	33–35
3T	29–33	36–38
4T	34–38	39–41

Size	Age	Height (inches)	Weight (pounds)
Newborn	3-6 months	21-23	12-17
Infant	6-12 months	24-28	18-22
XX-Small	12-18 months	28-31	22-27
X-Small	18 months-2 years	32-34	28-32
Small	2-3 years	35-38	32-35
Medium	3-4 yrs.	39-42	35-41 lbs.
Large	4-5 yrs.	42-46	41-50 lbs.

Metric Measures and Equivalents

Since most measurements that you receive from international adoptions are in metric increments, you will need a conversion chart. I included this one because I have had to refer to it several times.

Length

1 millimeter (mm)		= 0.0394 in.
1 centimeter (cm)	= 10 mm	= 0.3937 in.
1 meter (m)	= 1000 mm	= 1.0936 yd
1 kilometer (km)	= 1000 m	= 0.6214 mi.

Weight

1 milligram (mg)		= 0.0154 grain
1 gram (g)	= 1000 mg	= 0.0353 oz.
1 kilogram (kg)	= 1000 g	= 2.2046 lbs.
1 tonne (t)	= 1000 kg	= 1.1023 short tons or =0.9842 long ton

Area

1 sq. centimeter (cm. sq.)	= 100 mm sq.	= 0.155 sq. in.
1 sq. meter (m sq.)	= 10,000 cm sq.	= 1.1196 sq. yd
1 hectare (ha)	= 10,000 m sq.	= 2.4711 acres
1 sq. kilometer (km sq.)	= 100 ha	= 0.3861 sq. mi.

Volume

1 cubic centimeter (cm^3)		= 0.061 in^3
1 cubic decimeter (dm^3)	= 1000 cm^3	= 0.0353 ft^3
1 cubic meter (m^3)	= 1000dm^3	= 1.3079 yd^3
1 liter (L)	= 1 dm^3	= 0.2642 gal
1 hectoliter (hL)	=0 100 L	= 2.8378 bu

Temperature
Celsius = 5/9 (F-32 degrees)
Fahrenheit = 9/5 (C+32 degrees)

Celsius	-25	-18	-10	0	10	20	30	40
Fahrenheit	-13	0	14	32	50	68	86	104

Climate and Culture

Once you have a rough estimate of what size your child is, you will have to determine what your child's needs are. One of the largest factors affecting your child's clothing needs is whether your adoption is an international or domestic adoption. Internationally adopted children are usually smaller than their peers in the United States, especially if they have been in an orphanage. You also need to consider weather, climate, season, accuracy of available size information, cultural requirements, and the child's age.

As is the case in most international adoptions, your child will leave the orphanage wearing the clothes that you bring for her. You will probably want this to be a special outfit; it will be the one you have the first pictures taken in, pictures that you'll cherish forever. You will want to make sure that this outfit and the rest of the clothing that you bring for your child are seasonally appropriate and are in accordance with the customs of your host country. These customs could include wearing hats, not wearing shorts, or always wearing long sleeves. Remember, your child's caregivers will be observing you, and they want to make sure you are dressing the child appropriately.

Easy-Access Clothing

You may want to avoid clothing that has lots of buckles, buttons, snaps, or zippers. As a new parent, this will only add to your frustration when you are trying to learn to dress a moving target or undress one quickly. I like to avoid "onesies" and other one-piece clothing with snaps, especially for toddlers who are at least partially potty trained. Remember: you want easy-access, no-fuss clothing.

We had custody of our daughter for less than forty-eight hours when we returned to the United States. During the first leg of our trip, which included a ninety-minute flight to Moscow and a quick stop at a photographer's office before her embassy visit, she wore three dresses and two or three diapers.

Trying to get a sick toddler, whom we'd only had custody of for twelve hours, into an airplane bathroom to change her dirty diaper and clothing was quite an enlightening experience. Add to that trying to communicate with flight attendants who only spoke Russian that our daughter needed a sick bag, and you get an idea of our predicament. Thank goodness it was summer and our daughter was wearing was a knit dress and disposable training pants. New foods and new sensations helped contribute to her upset stomach, vomiting, and diarrhea.

To help determine how much clothing you will need, you need to take into consideration how long you will be in your host country with your child and what laundry options are available. Fortunately, we had same-day service for laundry at the hotels where we stayed.

I did feel sorry for the guard at the U.S. Embassy who had to check my diaper bag. In addition to a soiled dress, I had forgotten, in my panic, to replace the lid on Callie's cup and it had spilled juice everywhere.

The Basic Wardrobe

You will probably need to take a minimum of five outfits for your child. I recommend taking two outfits that should fit according to the available size information, two to three outfits that are the next size up, and maybe one that is a size smaller. You will probably want to take clothing that can be layered or mixed and matched. Consider the following clothing options:

- Boots and galoshes
- Dresses, jumpers
- Hair bows/barrettes
- Hats, scarves, gloves/mittens
- Jacket/coat or snowsuit
- Jeans or pants
- Pants/short sets
- Shoes, socks or tights
- Sweaters
- T-shirts, undershirts
- Turtlenecks, shirts, blouses
- Underwear/disposable training pants or diapers

Until you actually see your child in person, you probably will not want to purchase a large amount of clothing. To save on expenses, buy clothing from consignment shops, accept hand-me-downs, and borrow clothes from friends. Once you're home, fill in the wardrobe gaps. Don't over purchase—most likely your child will have a growth surge his first year home.

This simple outline helps provide the minimum basics until you return home. Interchange summer and winter items as necessary.

Girl's Basic Wardrobe
1 special outfit
1 dress
1 jumper and blouse
2 pants sets
1 or 2 turtlenecks or knit tops
1 pair of casual shoes
6 pairs of socks or tights
6 pairs of underwear
1 sweater or cardigan
Hair bows or hats

Boy's Basic Wardrobe
1 special outfit
2 pants sets
2 pairs of jeans or khaki pants
4 knit shirts or turtlenecks
1 pair sneakers or casual shoes
6 pairs of socks
6 pairs of underwear
1 sweater or jacket
Hats or caps

Chapter 5

The Nursery

I believe the process of planning a nursery is similar to that of planning a wedding. For years you've dreamed about it—picked colors, picked a theme, and imagined the big day when you bring your child home. Planning your future with your child is no different than planning a future with your spouse, make the most of it and enjoy this wonderfully frantic time.

The first thing I did was to decide which colors I would use in the nursery. After spending hours and eventually taking my husband on a shopping excursion (I was getting desperate), we finally decided on a comforter set that ultimately determined the color as well as the theme for the nursery: multicolored pastels with moons and stars. After you decide what colors and theme you want for your nursery, you are ready for the essentials.

A Crib or a Bed?

Because your toddler will not use a crib for the usual length of time, from infancy through the transition to a toddler or larger bed, I think the smart choice is a bed that can convert from a crib to a toddler bed. The bed I chose converts from a crib to a toddler bed and then to a full-size bed. Choose a bed that can convert to two different mattress heights when used as a crib. For a toddler, the bed would probably be used at the lowest setting; you many never need the upper setting.

In our case, we started the adoption process to adopt a fifteen-month-old toddler and ended up with a three-year-old. For our first child, we skipped the crib stage and went straight to the toddler daybed. For future children, infant or young toddler, we will be able to use the crib setting. A crib would have only been usable for another infant. Our daughter slept in a regular bed at the time of the adoption. It was not as big or as tall as a twin bed. It was a more like a modified toddler bed with no side rails. At 34 inches and 26½ pounds, she was technically small enough to fit in a crib, but she could have easily climbed out. She also grew 6 inches within the first year home.

The philosophy of when to move a toddler from a crib is subjective. Some people say when your child is 35 inches tall, she should be moved to a toddler or regular-size bed. Others say at thirty months of age or when the toddler starts climbing out of the crib. To be safe, check manufacturer's guidelines when purchasing the bed. Although some toddlers are probably large enough to skip the crib and go straight to a toddler or regular-size bed, many internationally adopted children are small for their age and are developmentally delayed.

I liked the idea of having the extra protection of a crib as a "containment field" while we adjusted to having a mobile toddler in the house while we were asleep. Crib extenders can be purchased if the crib's sides are not high enough.

Sleeping Arrangements

If possible, try to find out what type of bed your child is sleeping in now and what her sleeping arrangements are. For internationally adopted toddlers, sleeping customs will vary by culture. Eastern European children adopted from orphanages may have never slept in a room by themselves, and Asian children frequently sleep on a mattress on the floor. Children from South America may have slept in hammocks, while children from other parts of the world may sleep in the same bed as their caregivers.

Find out as much information about sleeping arrangements as you can. This will help you plan ahead for disruptive sleep patterns and ease any sleep discomfort or distress. Healthy infants and young or small toddlers should be placed on their backs to sleep. This will reduce the risk of Sudden Infant Death Syndrome (SIDS).

Overseas travel can result in jet lag. A newly arrived toddler may not be adjusted to the difference in time zones and may want to sleep all day and "party all night." She may have to be eased into sleeping in a crib, sleeping by herself, or sleeping in a dark or quiet room. You will probably learn by trial and error. Be prepared to have new arrivals sleep with you at least for the first few nights you are home.

Often parents of toddlers who have problems sleeping at night are told to let them cry it out. This technique is not appropriate for adopted toddlers who are insecurely attached. Allowing an adopted toddler who is not securely attached to his parents to cry it out can impede the attachment process.

We were lucky; our daughter took two naps, which equaled sleeping half of the trip home, and had no problem adjusting to the time change. She also slept in her own bed, starting with a nap on the first day home. I could tell that she was initially anxious about sleeping alone in her room, but we have never had any sleep issues except when we have been on vacation or in a different surrounding. New places and new beds mean Mommy may have to be in the room and we may have to use a nightlight.

Nursery Essentials

Here is a list of essential items for your nursery:

- Baby monitor
- Baby-size pillow
- Bed rail (if using a regular bed instead of a crib)
- Blankets
- Changing table
- Changing table pad
- Comforter set
- Crib bumper pad
- Crib or bed
- Diaper stacker
- Dresser
- Mattress
- Rocking chair
- Sheets

When choosing furniture (the crib, dresser, changing table, rocking chair), think ahead. Ask yourself if it's something you can use for a second child, if the color is neutral, if it's convertible, if it can be used in a different room later. The crib we chose converts from a toddler to a full-size bed, and the changing table is a short dresser fitted with a changing pad. When your child outgrows a changing table or you find that you don't use it, simply remove the changing pad.

Callie's bedroom set is a neutral light pine. A white bedroom set would have been beautiful in our nursery, but it wouldn't have been practical to use for a boy. You may also want to choose neutral colors for the nursery, especially for items that can be used again such as the changing pad, sheets, and blankets. One couple went to the Ukraine to adopt a girl and came home with a boy! They would have been in trouble if they had set up the nursery in pink ruffles. With adoption, things can change quickly and unexpectedly. Be flexible. It's more important to pick the right child than to pick a child who matches the nursery.

The crib mattress should be firm and should fit the crib snugly so that no more than two fingers fit between the mattress and the crib. A firm mattress will help keep the crib sheets in place, too. Crib slats should not be more than two inches apart. If your child starts out in a daybed rather than a crib, you may want to use a bed rail to help prevent falls.

Most infant comforter sets include one set of sheets, a comforter, a bumper pad, and a diaper stacker. I consider a diaper stacker optional and probably would not have bought one had it not been included in my set. Crib bumpers should not be used once your toddler can pull himself up on top of them, because they can be used as steps to climb out of the crib. Baby pillows are optional depending on the age and developmental level of your child and should be used with discretion. You may want to buy individual bedding pieces rather than buying a comforter set. Depending on your toddler's age, you may not be able to use all the components of a set.

When I registered for my baby shower, I requested one set of sheets in addition to those that came in the comforter set. It wasn't until later that I looked at a baby registry checklist and saw their recommendation of at least three or four sets of sheets. I picked four baby blankets in different fabrics and weights. I also picked an additional blanket in a light jersey knit that could be packed in a diaper bag or played with. We take it everywhere.

Consider the layout of your house. You may need a baby monitor in your nursery if your house is two stories, if the bedrooms are not close together, or if the bedrooms are removed from the main living space. Each child is different and some will need more supervision than others will when they are alone in their rooms.

Wall and Window Treatments

Wall and window treatments in the nursery may include the following:

•Blinds or shades
•Lamp(s)

- •Nightlight
- •Pictures
- •Wall hangings
- •Window treatments

Your toddler probably has the least amount of supervision while he is in the bed. Check the crib's placement in the nursery. Make sure that he can't reach wall hangings, pictures, or mirrors. A toddler can pull down pictures and mirrors on top of himself and get caught or tangled in wall hangings. Furniture placement is also important because a toddler can use other pieces of furniture to climb out of the crib. Check the outside area around the crib; you don't want your child to land on anything that could hurt him once he figures out how to escape from the crib.

While our daughter has always slept through the night, she would not get out of her bed without permission because of her orphanage training. She had been home over a year before she understood that it was okay to get up in the morning or if she needed to go to the bathroom. Her friend Vika, who was adopted at two-and-a-half years old, was just the opposite. Her mother frequently found that she had been out of the bed or was out of the bed when she checked on her. All toys, books, and the chest of drawers were fair game when Vika was out of bed. Make sure any toys with small parts and baby products are out of reach.

Blinds and shades should be lead-free. If your blinds are old, they may not be lead-free, and the dust buildup on them could include lead particles. Use a cord wind-up should be used on blinds to prevent the possibility of accidents involving tangled cords. Mobiles should not be used on toddler cribs; however, there are some crib toys that you may be able to use if you wish. Check the manufacturer's recommendation; this should tell you if it would be safe for your toddler to use them.

Lamps and nightlights should be out of a toddler's reach because both are burn hazards. Use cord roll-ups for lamps and other items with electrical cords to prevent toddlers from pulling these items off on top of them by the cord.

Miscellaneous

- Chew guard
- Clothes hangers and hamper
- Humidifier/vaporizer
- Memory box
- Pacifier
- Picture frames and album
- Pillow pal
- Small laundry bag
- Snugglies
- Teething ring

Your new toddler may not need a pacifier, but she may still be cutting teeth. A teething ring can help soothe sore teeth and gums. A chew guard will help protect your toddler's teeth as well as prevent damage to the crib.

You may need hangers for your child's clothing. I bought a small mesh laundry bag, made for small delicate items, to put our daughter's socks and tights in while they were in the washing machine. Her socks were so small I was afraid I would never find all the mates after I did laundry.

Picture frames, memory boxes, and picture albums will become treasured keepsakes. I couldn't find a baby book that I thought was appropriate for an adopted toddler. I chose a regular picture album, which also had two coordinating memory boxes and a video cover. I used the larger memory box for regular keepsakes and mementos. The smaller memory box I put aside for the special keepsakes that I want Callie to have when she is grown. The video cover is for the video of the first time we met her.

We have a small photo album that we used for photos of our trip. I wanted to be able to show our photos without them being mishandled. It is what I consider our "baby's first pictures." The album includes pictures of the three of us at the orphanage, sightseeing, and when we first arrived home. It is a treasured diary of our trip.

Pillow pals are animal-shaped pillows that can be used to play with or lie on in the crib or on the floor while watching TV. I like to think of them as functional stuffed animals that can be washed. (Check the manufacturer's label.) At night I sat our daughter's pillow pal in the floor next to her bed to help cushion her fall if she managed to get out of the crib. Snugglies, like pillow pals, can be used to help soothe toddlers; they are stuffed animals with a blanket body. A Snugglie eliminates the need for two separate items to search for.

After watching her cousin Kelsey with a treasured "baby," someone gave Callie one that was similar. She became instantly attached to this little pink bear and has slept with it at naptime and every night since. Losing this bear would be traumatic. I recommend purchasing an emergency backup for any well-loved "baby."

A humidifier or vaporizer is helpful for relieving stuffy noses caused by dry air. If you have central heat, you will probably want to invest in one to help prevent sleeplessness and wakeful toddlers.

Chapter 6

The Toy Box

No household would be complete without a wide assortment of toys, and your child will spend many happy hours playing with them. Choose toys that are appropriate for your child's developmental age rather than those for his chronological age. Toys for children over three may not be appropriate for newly adopted three-year-olds. They may not know not to put small parts in their mouths, and these toys may be too complex for them to play with as intended.

Your child may have little experience with toys or may have only been allowed to play with a few. Do not be surprised if you have to show him how to play with many of the toys that you have. Too many toys or a room full of toys may be overwhelming for a newly adopted toddler. Start slowly and follow his lead.

Beginning Basics

Blocks, balls, and container toys are great first toys for children. They stimulate children to reach for them and help teach manipulation, spatial relations, and hand-and-eye coordination. Toys should stimulate mental association, play familiar tunes, and help teach object permanence. Toddlers will enjoy stacking, throwing, and putting things in and dumping them out of containers.

Toddlers are drawn to light and sound and any toys that have buttons, bells, or whistles. Most will enjoy anything that plays music. Musical instruments such as pianos, xylophones, drums, or tambourines will provide your toddler with hours of fun.

Hide-and-seek, peak-a-boo, and patty-cake are favorite games. As your toddler becomes more mobile, push/pull toys such as cars, doll strollers, shopping carts, cars or animals with a pull cord, mini cars, lawnmowers, or other toys that imitate familiar everyday activities will be favorites.

Toys for Older Toddlers

Older toddlers will acquire new skills such as matching or sorting objects by size and color, recognizing numbers and letters, and fine motor skills. Puzzles, memory matching games, videos, books, and refrigerator magnets with ABCs and numbers are fun and educational.

Ring-around-the-rosy, itsy-bitsy spider, and "the wheels on the bus" will become familiar favorites. Children learn by imitation and will want to mimic the activities of others. They will want to cook, serve food, drive, clean house, or feed their babies.

As older toddlers become more mobile, you will have to take more precautions in your home. Flowerpots might become sandboxes and toilets might be used as a bathtub for a doll. While getting ready to attend a citizenship party for adopted children hosted by our congressional representative, Jim DeMint, I finished applying my makeup only to look down and find Callie had applied her own lipstick. At least she picked red, which coordinated with her dress. Anything within a toddler's reach is fair game and you will find that they are quite ingenious.

Baby Dolls and Snuggly Toys

Except for rare occasions, Callie did not want to sleep with any of her dolls or stuffed animals in the bed. That all changed when she met Baby Bear, a little pink stuffed bear that is actually a baby toy with a rattle inside. Since she received her "baby," she has become very attached to it and has not slept a single night without it. Because she is so attached, I found a backup in case something ever happened to her beloved little bear. I also bought a green one for her to give to her little brother when he came home.

I like stuffed animals that are soft and fluffy. These are great for kids to snuggle with, and I especially like ones that can be washed. I do not care for many of the ones that sing or dance and need batteries. They are not soft; they are not washable and are not particularly toddler-proof.

One of Callie's favorite dolls is Zoë, which has clothes that button, snap, and tie. Another is her *kookla* ("doll" in Russian), which was the closest thing to handmade that I could find. This was the doll that we gave her when she left the orphanage. Callie also has a lifesize doll that has red hair the same color as a friend at school. She likes to carry her around the house.

Any type of doll brings out the maternal instinct in Callie. She will rock, sing to, feed, and drive them in their stroller. Thanks to Gramma, she has the deluxe baby stroller complete with baby carrier. Of course, she also has baby clothes, bottles, and brushes. She has lots of dishes, and her babies are well fed. She is quite the hostess and frequently serves tea from her tiny silver tea set that her Aunt Merry gave her.

Using Toys for Teaching

If your child will be in a new environment or, as in our daughter's case, requires hospitalization and surgery, toys can help prepare them by familiarizing them with the objects or location in which they will be exposed. Before Callie had surgery, we purchased the *Sesame Street Visits the Hospital* video. We also bought a medical kit. It is still a favorite toy for the future "Dr. Hoppenhauer," who really likes to give people shots. Because Callie would be required to wear arm splints for at least a week after her surgery, we played hospital with a stuffed bear. At the advice of Alex's mom, who had done the same thing for him, Mr. Bear had to wear bandages and arm splints. He also had his temperature taken, his mouth and ears checked, his heart and lungs listened to, his blood pressure taken, and more. This type of play can help children feel more comfortable in new situations—especially a place as scary as the hospital.

Teaching with toys or role-playing with them can put a child at ease and help her have a better understanding of a situation, even if she can't fully appreciate what is happening or if there is a language barrier.

Children's Books

I can't say enough about books. Books are one of my favorite gifts for children. I believe that storybooks and reading to your children, as well as books that teach, help set the foundation for further education and learning. They also help increase vocabulary, improve reading comprehension, and instill a desire and the ability to continue to learn.

If your child doesn't speak English, reading to him will help him learn the language. One book that I bought for our toddler was the *Fisher-Price Wordbook*. It contained more than 500 words, complete with illustrations. I brought it when we went to Russia. I thought the pictures would help keep Callie entertained while she got a lesson in English. Although this book was probably meant for toddlers, I believe it could also be used for children up to six years of age.

One of my all-time favorite children's books is Dr. Seuss's *The Cat in the Hat Beginner Book Dictionary*. This book has examples of words that begin with each letter of the alphabet. Each word is illustrated and accompanied by a sentence that uses the word. I can't tell you how many times I referred to this dictionary when I wanted to draw something that was illustrated in it. No child should be without this book.

I took Sesame Street coloring books and Little Golden Books to the orphanage and was told that Russian children are not exposed to *Sesame Street*. They referred to the Sesame Street characters as monsters (a term I'm sure that the "monsters" on "Sesame Street" would not object to). We were also told that the children are not used to seeing characters but use real animals and people for their stories. I have since heard that the Teletubbies have infiltrated Russian television, and some children have gotten to watch these in the orphanage.

Books that involve naming or moving body parts, numbers, or colors will help keep your active toddler occupied while teaching them new words. In my effort to keep our daughter bilingual, I learned all the names of the body parts in Russian and read them to her in both Russian and English.

One of the many books I bought our daughter was *The First Thousand Words in Russian* by Amery, Kirienko, and Cartwright. This book contains pictures of everyday scenes, accompanied by the word in Russian and followed by the pronunciation. It is also available in English, French, German, Spanish, Italian as well, and can be purchased from Barnes and Noble. Callie is too young to use it now, but I hope that she will enjoy it as she gets older.

You may also be able to find a variety of books that take place in or are about your child's native country. Some of these may have to be specially ordered from adoption-related Web sites. Both the Eloise and Madeline children's book characters are international travelers. Eloise visits Moscow while Madeline spends time with Gypsies in France. Although most of these books would be too advanced for a toddler, you may want to make a mental note to buy them later.

Educational Toys, Videos, Tapes, and CDs

When we adopt a child, we often find that we adopt our child's country and culture. World history has always been of interest, and I find that multiculturalism is now a favorite subject. There are a variety of language and educational materials available for children that help promote this multiculturalism.

Bilingual Baby and *Teach Me* tapes are just two of the children's cassettes that are available in many different languages. Some teach words or phrases while others contain songs or nursery rhymes. When we purchased the *Teach Me Russian* cassette, we discovered one of Callie's favorite songs was on the tape. She would make special facial expressions when the song was played.

"Language Littles" are bilingual dolls available in Spanish, Italian, French, Mandarin, Japanese, Russian and more. Each sixteen-inch doll speaks between twenty-five and thirty phrases in English and another language. New dolls are currently being added to this collection.

See 'n' Say Kids Around the World by Fisher-Price is a great toy. It teaches words, phrases, counting, music, geography, and facts about the world. It features fifteen different countries including Russia, Mexico, the United States, China, India, and Kenya.

Large Toys and Outdoor Toys

Most children enjoy a rocking horse, play table and chairs, an art easel, or a kitchen set. I especially like a kitchen set and found that many toddlers will play with one for hours.

Callie enjoys jumping on a mini trampoline and has used it so much that she has built up very strong muscles in her legs. Other outdoor toys that are fun for toddlers include a swing set, play pool, and sandbox complete with bucket and pail. Wagons, push cars, and tricycles are other favorites.

Chapter 7

Child Safety

There are many ways to protect your child from harm. Common sense and child awareness can be two of your best lines of defense. While it is impossible to eliminate the threat of accidents completely, you can significantly reduce the opportunity for dangerous and potentially life-threatening conditions. It is your responsibility as a parent to do so.

Keep the telephone numbers for your pediatrician, poison control center, Ask-a-Nurse programs, local emergency response line, and other related services posted close to the telephone.

Toddlers are inquisitive by nature but lack an understanding of cause and effect. It takes just a few seconds for a toddler to get into trouble. Seemingly harmless conditions that can increase your toddler's risk for accident include the following:

- Busy time of day
- Change in routine or caregivers
- Death in the family
- Hunger (the hour before dinnertime)
- New addition to the family (child or pet)
- New home

•One or both parents out of town
•Parent(s)/caretaker(s) who are preoccupied: talking on the telephone, watching TV or working on the computer
•Parental stress
•Parents or caregivers in the bathroom
•Parents separating, divorcing or experiencing marital difficulties
•Pregnancy
•Preparing for, traveling to, and being on vacation
•Sibling has recently had an accident resulting in injury or broken bones
•Sick parent or siblings

Danger Zones

To childproof your home, start by placing any breakables, collectibles, and dangerous or irreplaceable items out of your toddler's reach. Toilets, stairs, and electrical appliances pose a great threat to your toddler, as do medications and household cleaners. The most common accidents for toddlers include climbing, poisoning, drowning, auto accidents, and cuts and abrasions.

Zone 1: Medications

All medications should have childproof lids and should be kept safely out of reach. Medicine cabinets are unsafe because they rarely lock and can be reached by a climbing toddler. Sharp objects like scissors, razors, and pins should be removed from unlocked medicine cabinets.

Zone 2: Water

Toilets, tubs, whirlpools, and buckets or other water-filled containers, including ice chests and diaper pails, all pose a threat to your toddler. Buckets that hold five gallons or more are the most dangerous. Toddlers are top-heavy and can get stuck in any of these receptacles. You should never leave a toddler unattended in a bath or near any body of water. It only takes a few inches of water to drown in.

Zone 3: Edibles

Many common household cleaners are poisonous if ingested. To minimize the risk of toddlers ingesting these substances, always keep cleaning supplies in a securely locked area. These also need to be kept out of reach while you are using them. Always keep syrup of ipecac handy (to induce vomiting) and near the number for the poison hot line. BE sure to call the hot line, however, before you give your child ipecac. Some poisons may do more damage when regurgitated.

Leaving the most cautious toddler alone even for a few minutes when using household cleaners could be dangerous. Toddlers can be easily tempted by the pretty blue window cleaner that looks like the fruity drink the nice person brings them at the restaurant. Cocktails, beer, or wine are also fair game for toddlers and could result in intoxication or an alcohol overdose. Always empty glasses when you finish and teach toddlers that they are not to drink after other people.

Zone 4: The Garage

When you childproof your home, don't forget the garage. Paint, pesticides, and fertilizers can be toxic if ingested. Tools should also be left unplugged and out of reach. If you have an automatic garage door opener, check to see how well the door stops and what size triggers it. I saw a test on television that suggested putting a cantaloupe or other melon where the garage door closes. If the melon is crushed, the garage door is a safety threat to your child.

Zone 5: Climbing

As your toddler enters the climbing stage, anything he can step on, pull up on, or climb on top of is potentially dangerous. Stairs should have gates at the top as well as the bottom. Bookcases, dressers, or other pieces of furniture should be bolted to the wall if it they are not secure enough to prevent your toddler from pulling them.

I use what I call the "finger test." I placed four fingers from each hand approximately 1½ to 2 inches from the edge of the furniture in question. If I think the furniture could be pulled over with the light amount of pressure I applied, then I took safety precautions. It was just my luck that the only piece of furniture I deemed unsafe in our house was the tall dresser in the nursery.

Zone 6: Electrical Appliances

Electrical appliances should always be turned off after use and kept out of reach. A toddler should never be allowed to touch an electrical appliance in the bathroom (hair dryer, curling iron, etc.) or in any other area that is close to water. Appliances that are plugged in do not have to be turned on to cause electrocution if they are exposed to or submerged in water. Irons can remain hot after use and should never be left on an ironing board. When moving a hot iron to a secured area, make sure the electrical cord is not left dangling and is also out of reach. Electrical cords for lamps, appliances, and so on, should be hidden or out of reach. This will prevent your toddler from pulling appliances on top of herself or possibly getting cut or burned.

Home Safety

No home could be properly childproofed without a variety of safety devices. You will have to assess your surroundings to determine which items best suit your needs. Items you may need to childproof your home include:

•Baby monitor
•Childproof patio door lock

•Choke tube
•Cord wind-ups
•Corner guards
•Door alarms
•Doorknob guards
•Door locks
•Doorstops
•Drawer locks
•Fire extinguisher
•Nonskid tub mats
•Outlet covers
•Playpen
•Power strip safety cover
•Safety gate/stair guard
•Screen guard
•Skid-resistant/tip-resistant stepstool
•Smoke alarm
•Stove guard
•Stove knob covers
•Toilet lid lock
•Tub spout covers
•VCR guard

Socket Safety

Outlet covers should cover electrical sockets. I recently saw a power outlet without covers next to a sink. Since this is well within reach of wet little hands, it is an accident waiting to happen.

If you use power strips, invest in a power strip safety cover. Cord wind-ups will help prevent children from pulling on electrical cords or pulling electrical appliances over.

Doors and Windows

If you have louvered doors or doors without locks, you may need to invest in door locks to keep toddlers out of these rooms or closets. Kid-proof patio door locks are also available for screen doors, which frequently do not have locks.

Check window screens. I was at a friend's house recently when the screen fell out of one of her windows. You may need to purchase screen guards to prevent toddlers from falling out or climbing out of windows.

Venetian blinds should have cord wind-ups installed so your toddler cannot become tangled in excess cord.

You may need door lock covers so that your toddler cannot lock himself in or you out of a room. This happens more often in a bathroom than any other room. This will of course present a whole other set of dangers, especially if you are visiting someone else's home. Toddlers are sometimes able to lock a door but have trouble unlocking it. I was once locked out of a house by a three-year-old that I was babysitting. It took a lot of coaxing to be allowed back into the house. If your toddler climbs out of bed at night or if he is a sleepwalker, all doors leading to the outside need door lock covers.

If you have a security system in your home, you may want to consider door alarms. They will tell you when someone enters or leaves the house and which door they are using. This will prevent toddlers from escaping unnoticed.

The Bathroom

No bathroom would be complete without a fair amount of safety devices. You should purchase a toilet lid lock to help keep toddlers out of the toilet, and your bathtub should have faucet covers and nonskid tub mats. These will help prevent falls and injury from toddlers bumping their heads on faucets. Most likely your toddler will need a stepstool to reach the sink. Stepstools should be skid- and tip-resistant. Medicine cabinets as well as other cabinets or drawers that contain household cleaners, medication, baby products (don't forget about any that may be in a toddler's bedroom), cosmetics, razors, scissors should have drawer and cabinet locks.

The Kitchen

Stove knob covers prevent your toddler from being able to turn the stove off or on. When cooking, use back burners whenever possible so toddlers won't be tempted to grab pot handles. When our daughter was in the hospital after she had her palate repaired, there was another child in the hospital who had pulled a pot of green beans on top of himself, resulting in serious burns. A stove guard could have prevented that accident.

Drawer and cabinet locks and latches should be used anywhere there are items that could cause injury to a toddler. Cutlery, scissors, or other sharp objects should be out of reach. If your toddler has ever been in a situation where having enough food to eat was an issue, you may need to put a lock on the pantry to prevent unsupervised bingeing or "stealing" food.

Corner Guards

Corner guards are especially important in preventing injuries to toddlers. Coffee tables, end tables, and countertops can cause injury if a toddler hits her head on one. A neighbor's child hit her head on the corner of a piano and ended up starting school with two black eyes. The school called the Department of Social Services, and it led to an investigation.

Choke Tube

One way to test whether an object is too small for your toddler to play with or needs to be stored out of his reach is to test it in a choke tube. A choke tube is an acrylic tube that helps determine what represents a choking hazard. If the object will fit into the tube, it could be a choking hazard. Many small items are marked "not for children under 3." Because internationally adopted children may be small for their age or developmentally behind, you may need to consider if your child is big enough or mature enough to play with these items as they were intended.

VCR Guard

One of the newest child safety products is the VCR guard. Actually this item is really a VCR safety device since it protects the VCR from your child! A VCR guard will prevent your toddler from inserting movies or other foreign objects into the VCR. Recently, at a friend's home the VCR was the first thing our daughter went for because it was within her reach. She is just now close to reaching our VCR at home and has made several attempts to insert a movie herself.

Fire Safety

All homes should have smoke detectors and fire extinguishers. Check periodically to make sure they are in working order. All children's pajamas should be flame resistant. Pajamas should fit snugly and be free of damage like rips or tears or missing or loose buttons. It is much safer for your child to sleep in pajamas rather than T-shirts or other favorite articles of clothing. Your home should have window decals alerting rescue personnel that there are children or pets in the home. These decals are usually available from the fire department.

The Playpen

If for some reason you need to divert your complete attention to something besides your toddler, a playpen can be used temporarily to keep her out of trouble. Although you would not want to leave her in the playpen for any length of time, it can come in handy if the phone rings, your dinner is burning, or you need to go to the bathroom. We have a portable playpen that also makes a great little travel bed. It also keeps toddlers from wandering off in a strange place.

Car Seats

Toddlers—or infants, for that matter—should *never* be left alone in a car—even for a few minutes—and keys should never be left in the ignition. When you load your car with groceries or other items, your child should always be the last thing that goes into the car.

When selecting a new car seat, make sure the one you select meets federal motor vehicle safety standards. If you will be using the car seat on an airplane, it should meet FAA requirements. Five-point harnesses provide more protection than three-point harnesses. According to the American Academy of Pediatrics, "Do not use shield boosters for children under 40 pounds, even if they are labeled for use at a lower weight."

Toddlers and young children should always ride in weight-appropriate car seats. When choosing a car seat for your toddler, you may want to consider how long your child will be able to use it and if it can be handed down to a younger sibling. We were lucky because the car seat we chose could be used for children weighing five to forty pounds. Since our daughter was almost thirty pounds when we adopted her, she was not able to use it for very long. However, our second addition would, and we planned on moving Callie to a new seat upon his arrival or when she outgrew, whichever came first.

Car seats are safest when placed in the backseat. If possible, use the middle seat; it is the safest. A significant amount of car seats are installed incorrectly. To protect your child, have your car seat installation checked by an expert. Many police departments, fire departments, and automobile companies provide this service for free. Even when your toddler is buckled into a car seat, there is no guarantee that he can't escape. Teach your toddler proper etiquette for riding in a car: no screaming, no throwing things, and keep the seat belt on. You may want to keep a towel handy to cover any metal or plastic that could become hot while your car is sitting in the sun.

We bought a car seat under mat help protect the car from accidents; it has a mesh pocket to store toys or other essentials. We also were given a baby view mirror. It has a suction cup that attaches to the windshield and allows you to see into the backseat so you can check on your toddler as often as needed.

Strollers

Choose a stroller that will provide your child with the best protection. A stroller should have a wide wheelbase to prevent tipping. Check for under-seat storage, because hanging a purse or diaper bag on stroller handles can cause tipping.

The frame should not have sharp edges or spaces that could trap fingers and toes. The stroller should also have durable straps that can be adjusted and opened easily only by adults. Brakes are also important to prevent the stroller from rolling.

When shopping for a stroller, check out its weight and ease of use. Will you be able to pick it up and use it on your own? This is especially important if you are adopting more than one child and need a double or triple stroller. If you are adopting an infant and toddler consider a double stroller, that has a standard stroller seat, a space for older toddlers/kindergartners to stand, and a small benchseat.

Depending on the size of your toddler and your needs, you may be able to purchase a convertible stroller/car seat, thus eliminating the need for two separate items.

I like using an umbrella stroller. We chose a modified, more durable "sport-utility stroller." It has a retractable canopy, a storage basket, eight-inch wheels, and it opens and closes easily. Many great stroller accessories are also available, including drink holders, food trays, and holders for toys and other gadgets.

Less expensive strollers are lightweight and can be kept in your car for quick and easy access and can be used alternately with a more heavy-duty stroller. They can be found in most discount or baby stores and usually retail for around $15 to $20.

Baby Carriers and Slings

Baby carriers, slings, and other baby-wearing devices are very popular. They can help bonding and attachment while making life more convenient for new parents. Parents of small toddlers should be able to use some of these products.

The Baby Bjorn front carrier is for birth to ten months, or 8 to 33 pounds. While a front carrier may fit, it may be more constrictive than a small wiggly toddler would like.

Hip Hammocks or other slings help with the natural tendency to carry a child sideways on the hip. They are designed for a slightly older baby/toddler and can be used by children who are 14 to 35 pounds and two months to three years old.

Baby carriers should hold and support the child and have proper back support for the carrier. Your child should not be able to get out of the restraints or slip through the leg holes.

Use caution when wearing toddlers as they can and will pick up things that they are not supposed to. Toddlers are also more likely to wiggle, stand up, or try to get out of their carrier. It may be necessary to do back-strengthening exercises before using one.

Carriers may come in handy if you are doing a large amount of walking. You cannot run with a baby in these. Avoid running while carrying a small child in any manner; it can cause shaken baby syndrome. You can, however, run while pushing them in a jog stroller.

Safety Harness

Harnesses for children should be used sparingly and with caution. Both parent and child should be attached to each other, rather than the parent holding a leash. Resist the urge to pull on the cord to prevent misconduct or to change directions. This could result in your child falling or receiving other injury.

Harnesses are useful if you are shopping, attending a crowded festival, at an amusement park, or have several small children to watch, or if your child has a tendency to run ahead and hide.

Safety harnesses are not appropriate to use when traveling overseas to complete an adoption. While they are somewhat controversial in the United States, they are considered completely inappropriate elsewhere and could result in an adoption backlash within your host country.

Safety Resources

You may request safety information from the following resources:

- •Nationwide Poison Control Center: (800) 222-1222
- •U.S. Consumer Product Safety Commission's Hot Line: (800) 638-2772
- •Juvenile Products Manufacturers Association: They have safety certification on many baby products, including information on cribs, high chairs, walkers, and stoppers. Send a self addressed, stamped envelope to:
  Juvenile Products Manufacturers Association
  2 Greentree Center, Suite 225
  PO Box 955
  Marlton, NJ 08053
- •Injury Prevention Program: Information is available from the American Academy of Pediatrics on childproofing your home. (800) 433-9016

•For the <u>Family Shopping Guide to Car Seats</u>, send a self-addressed, stamped envelope to:
AAP, Safe Ride Program
141 Northwest Point Blvd.
PO Box 927
Elk Grove Village, IL 60009-0927
•<u>The Auto Safety Hotline:</u> Call (800) 424-9393 for current information on child safety-seat recalls, safety notices, and replacement parts.

Chapter 8

A Safe Outdoors

Once you have childproofed your home, you will realize that the great outdoors presents a whole new set of problems. When outdoors, toddlers should never be left unsupervised. They should also be taught never to leave their specific play area without your permission.

If your yard is fenced, make sure all latches are in working order and that your toddler cannot unlatch them. At our house, we had imaginary lines at the sides of the house that Callie was not allowed past. We never allowed her in the front yard by herself when she was small.

Parking Lots and Streets

Set clear parameters for walking in parking lots and for crossing streets. Teach children not to play in the street or to cross the street by themselves. Always teach them to look left and right before crossing.

Our rules are simple:

1. No playing while getting in or out of the car, especially when it is dark.
2. You must hold a hand while in a parking lot or when you are crossing the street. If Callie refuses to hold my hand in the parking lot, then she loses walking privileges. We will simply pick her up and carry her (sometimes kicking and screaming) either to the car or to the sidewalk.

Water Safety

Water poses a potential threat to your toddler, and he should never be left unattended in or near hot tubs, swimming pools, ornamental garden ponds, or even kiddy pools. Toddlers can drown in only a few inches of water. Always follow strict water safety rules:

1. Swimming pools should be equipped with appropriate life-saving devices.
2. Pool covers do not provide the necessary safety that a fenced-in pool area provides.
3. Do not rely on flotation devices to protect your child completely.
4. Children of all ages and swimming abilities still need adult supervision.
5. No running by the pool.
6. Small children must wear safety devices the entire time they are in the pool area not just while in the water.
7. Children are not allowed to stand on the edge of an adult pool and get things out or scoop out water.
8. Always remove toys, floats, and so on from the pool after use.
9. Teach children that they are not allowed in the pool or pool area without an adult
10. Make sure there is always one adult present for every three children.

If you have a pool in your yard that has water over six feet deep and you cannot swim well enough to jump in after someone, then children should not be allowed in the pool area without an adult present who can.

Insects and Other Pests

Always take steps to protect your toddlers from insects. Children may be quite intrigued by a variety of bugs and assorted creepy-crawlies. You may even be given one as a "gift." You can teach your toddler to identify friendly or harmless insects from those that could potentially bite or sting.

It may be necessary to use an insect repellant to protect your child from mosquitoes during summer months. It is important to follow the manufacturer's guidelines and rinse repellants off when children return indoors.

Because you may have very little family history, you may not know if your child has a predisposition to being allergic to bee stings or other insect bites. You may want to keep children's Benadryl on hand or consult your pediatrician on how to best prepare for such an event.

If your child has been bitten or stung and is developing a rash or hives, call your pediatrician and seek medical help immediately. Your child could be having a potentially life-threatening allergic reaction.

Playgrounds and Parks

Swing sets and jungle gyms are great ways for children to learn new skills and spend time with their peers. For Callie's fourth birthday, she was given a swing set. It did not take her long to master swinging and she can swing as high as it will go. (You will be grateful when your child learns this skill and you don't have to push!) Anchors are a safety necessity to prevent swing sets from flipping, and most manufacturers recommend using either wood chips, mulch, or sand under playground equipment. Periodically check for loose nuts, bolts, or anything that could catch clothing or hair.

Playground safety is much like teenagers learning the rules of the road. Teach toddlers to wait until it is their turn to go down a slide. Children should never stand on, climb up, or push someone down a slide. Swing safety includes no jumping from swings, no swinging on stomachs, no walking in front of or behind someone who is swinging, no pushing peers, and no twisting chains on the swing.

When visiting neighborhood parks, make sure that you keep your child in view at all times. Examine the area to make sure there are no areas that need repair or that could cause injury to your child. In summer months, check that equipment is not too hot to burn your child. If you see something that is a potential safety hazard, report it to park management.

Sandboxes should have fresh, clean sand and be free of sticks, leaves, and other debris. Always keep sandboxes covered when not in use. Don't let your child throw or eat sand, no matter how delicious the mud pies look.

Cats and Dogs

Pets are extremely scent-oriented. As soon as we got our court date, I began wearing the baby lotion I had gotten for our daughter. My theory was that if our cat began associating this smell with me, when we arrived with our daughter he would be familiar with her scent and might more readily accept a new addition.

I also closed the door to the nursery to get the cat used to not being able to spend time in that room. After the cat discovered that the diaper-changing pad was a nice soft place to sleep, he then discovered that the crib was an even better place to sleep. My first thought was that it wasn't that big a deal since our three-year-old soon-to-be-daughter was big enough to move the cat if by some chance he jumped in the converted daybed with her. It then occurred to me that we had just signed papers on an infant due to be born in several months. The baby would be in the crib, not our three-year-old. The cat was immediately banned from the crib.

Toddlers may not understand the difference between pet food and people food. This is especially true of dry cat food. Children who have experienced hunger or malnutrition may be especially attracted to pet food. If it is kept in an easily accessible area or where the pet has continual access to his food bowl, your toddler may consider it fair game the next time he's hungry. When my brother was small (I love telling this story), I caught him eating dry cat food. (Of course, I immediately told on him.) You may need to reconsider your pet's feeding rituals and food location.

As soon as our cat and our daughter became familiar with each other, I began the process of helping the two of them bond. I had always poured the cat's dry food directly into the bowl, which was sitting in its usual location. After our daughter arrived, I would pick up the food bowl and fill it up. After the bowl was full, I would give it to our daughter and help her give it to the cat. This served the dual purpose of teaching our daughter that this food was for the cat and of helping the cat accept her as a member of the family. Now Callie and our cat are good friends, and the cat will even let her brush him.

Dogs often pose more of a threat to children than cats. Although both can bite, dog bites can be much more serious. Cat scratches can be nasty and can leave scars; however, the most serious pet-related injuries usually are a result of dog attacks. Dogs are pack animals and must establish dominance over—or be submissive to—newcomers.

Children who are new to the home and pet or are visiting should never be left unattended with a dog. This is especially important for medium to large dogs or for species that tend to be more aggressive like rottweilers, German shepherds, Doberman pinschers, and so on. If you have or know of a dog that has bitten children before, you need to take steps to protect both your toddler and the pet.

A friend's dalmatian not used to being around children bit her niece after she backed him into a corner. In many states, emergency room personnel are required by law to report these incidences. They must then be investigated and require quarantine of the animal to ensure they do not have rabies. If the animal repeats its actions and bites another child, regardless of the circumstances, it will be put to sleep as required by law.

You should teach your toddler the following pet etiquette, or "peti-quette" as I like to call it:

1. Ask a grownup for permission before approaching or petting an animal.
2. Avoid animals you do not know, and call a grownup if they approach you or enter your yard.
3. Never approach or touch a sleeping animal.
4. Never approach a mother animal with her babies without a grownup.
5. Do not touch an animal's food.
6. Do not poke an animal in the eyes.
7. Do not chase an animal that is running from you.
8. Leave fighting animals alone and call for a grownup.
9. If an animal is growling or angry, immediately stop what you are doing.

The first thing I do when I meet a new animal is to slowly reach out my hand and let him smell it. I figure that if he is clearly not interested, he will let me know by walking away or ignoring me. The correct way for a toddler to pet an animal is to rub it under the chin or to gently stoke his back. If a dog is growling or angry, the child should look down at his feet, take a step back and roll into a ball, covering his face with his arms. For an upset cat, the child should back away slowly. Usually a cat will then remove himself from the situation.

Other Animals

Cats and dogs are not the only pets that could pose a danger to your toddler. Hamsters, parakeets, lizards, skinks, monkeys, ferrets, rabbits, geese, and snakes will all bite. As a former zoo volunteer who helped with the two- and three-year-old classes, I know first-hand that toddlers have a natural tendency to go for animals' eyes. Eyes are located close to the mouth, and it is an animal's natural instinct to bite when it feels threatened. Virtually any animal cage that a toddler can get his fingers into can expose a toddler to potential injury.

Don't forget outdoor animals; this would include both wild animals and livestock. Most wild animals will run when approached by humans. That doesn't mean that toddlers will not pursue them. Given the opportunity, most toddlers will try to pick up or pet wild animals.

Large predators like a mountain lion will look for the smallest prey, if they decide to pursue a group of humans. Never let your toddler run ahead or lag behind when hiking or walking on trails. However, if a bear approaches your child, she should curl up into a little ball on the ground. But if she is approached by a large feline, she should grab the hem of her jacket and raise both the jacket and her arms over her head. This will make her appear larger and should make the predator second-guess its attack.

Although livestock are domesticated, that doesn't mean accidents don't happen. Just the size difference between a toddler and a horse or cow is an accident waiting to happen. Also be aware of water sources. Is the livestock's primary water source a pond or large trough that a toddler could get into? Is there a ladder in the barn leading to an open second level? Do electrical fences surround the animals, or can your toddler climb through the fence where the animals are?

Always be aware of your surroundings and potential hazards. Look for ways to prevent injuries. Teach your children to respect animals and their environment. Many zoos have classes available for toddlers and older children. These classes are a great way to introduce children to animals that they might not otherwise get the opportunity to meet.

Miscellaneous

Other potential hazards may include the following:

- Assorted tools (including garden tools)
- Buckets
- Chemicals for the pool
- Decks
- Driveway
- Electrical outlets
- Fences or gates
- Fertilizer, pesticides, or lawn chemicals
- Fireworks, including sparklers
- Holes
- Hot grills, matches, fire starters
- Lawnmowers
- Picnic tables, lawn chairs
- Plants, flowers, vegetables, berries
- Rocks
- Steps or ladders
- Trees (climbing)/tree houses
- Wells
- Woodpiles

Chapter 9

Mealtime Mania

I love toddlers. I love the way one day they will eat broccoli and the next day they won't. I love the way they say "yuck" when they try something new and how their version of trying a new food is to stick their tongue on it. I love their little pouty faces when you tell them no, how their eyes get as big as saucers when you bring them a present, and how they play with their silverware even when it regularly lands on the floor. I also love how you can make them laugh by just pretending to tickle them.

I believe that toddlers live in a world all their own. They are the center of their own universe, and we are the loyal subjects ready to attend to their every command. I have affectionately named this small kingdom of little people the Kingdom of Toddlerdom.

Not long before we adopted our daughter, a friend's toddler sat next to me at the dinner table and proceeded to scream "I want some juice" while kicking me under the table. What did we do? You guessed it; we got him some juice. Of course it didn't help that we had forgotten to get him something to drink.

Setting the Table

You will need some or all of the following:

•Baby bottles with nipples
•Bibs
•Booster chair
•Bottle brush
•Bottle warmer
•Dinnerware
•Food storage containers
•High chair
•Insulated bottle tote
•Silverware
•Splat mat
•Training cups

Your toddler's age, development, and current diet will help determine your dining needs. She may have eaten only semisolid foods or may not have been exposed to many different foods. Young toddlers or special-needs toddlers may still be bottle-fed. On the other hand, in many countries, children are weaned at an early age, and toddlers may have to learn how to use a sippy cup or straw.

The children at Callie's orphanage drank out of teacups. Because her cleft palate had not been repaired, Callie could not use a straw or a spill-proof cup if it had the spill-proof insert in place. Because of this, I did not know for several months that the insert was not supposed to be removed when in use.

Your child may never have eaten from a plate, never have used a fork or even had silverware for that matter. If the primary food was porridge, then she may have only used a bowl and spoon for eating. She may never have fed herself, eaten with her fingers, or been allowed to touch her food. You will learn from trial and error.

Being Seated

Don't buy one of those fancy, expensive high chairs that your toddler will not want to sit in after he figures out everyone else is in a big chair. The best buy for the amount of time you will use it is a four-way convertible high chair. The one that we purchased held an infant carrier. It also converted into a regular high chair. Once your child does not need to use the high chair tray and wants to sit at the table, the chair can be converted to a stand-alone booster chair and will also convert to a table and chair desk set, complete with a desk tray for storing crayons and paper.

When your child decides it is time to sit in a chair like a grownup (or other children), you may need to purchase a regular booster chair that will fit into your dining room chairs. The best product that we found was a portable booster seat. It folds down so you can take it with you out to dinner, on vacation, or to dinner at a friend's. Depending on the age or size of your toddler, you may be able to skip the high chair and purchase a booster chair. With Callie at age three, we certainly could have.

Spills Happen

The single, most important mealtime necessity is the Splat Mat. No matter what the seating arrangement is there will be spills and dropped food. This mat will save your carpet or flooring and make cleanup simple. Simply put this plastic floor cover beneath your child's seat and presto! An anti-carpet-cleaning device.

Short of an all-out food fight, your flooring will probably be spared. However, that dropped peanut butter and jelly sandwich may not always land where it is most convenient. If your home is carpeted, you will want to invest in a good spot remover.

The phrase "you are what you eat" must have came from the mother of a toddler. Toddlers, especially young toddlers who may be trying lots of new foods, will frequently wear their dinner. Your budding artist will love to touch, taste, finger-paint, and sculpt with his food.

Bibs will help protect and keep clothes clean. Cloth bibs can be thrown in the wash while waterproof bibs can be wiped off with a clean damp cloth. Disposable bibs are the latest invention; they would be great for traveling.

Of course any new parent knows that once a spot has made its way onto your beloved toddler's clothing, the clothes should be changed. Wrong! You will learn to overcome this temptation. It's okay. You will get used to it. You do not have to change your child's clothes immediately; at the rate of two or three shirts or outfits a day, you will soon learn that "spills happen."

Table Manners

Table manners will vary. Both Callie and her friend Victoria had great table manners when they came home. However, this did not last long for either child. Once they discovered that mealtime is a pleasant experience, where there are a variety of foods and there is always enough, their table manners deteriorated and they began to behave more like typical toddlers.

Your child may have had to fight to protect her food from other children, or she may have been an aggressor. Callie wanted all of her dinnerware to touch. She would eat all the crumbs off the table and wanted those on the floor as well. At first she would eat everything, but once she learned that she had options, there was always enough food, and she did not have to eat things she did not like, she became much more selective.

Victoria would put her arm around her plate as to not allow anyone else to get close, and Callie once pulled a hamburger out of my hand after I had taken it from her because the meat was about to fall out. For children in orphanages, mealtime was a serious business and there was never enough food.

A turning point for Callie was when she would eat a dozen or so bites and want to be excused. The small amount of food took the edge off of her hunger, and because she could comprehend the difference between being hungry and knowing true hunger, she did not want to finish her dinner. At that point she was confident that there was always enough food and that if she was hungry, she would be fed.

Once your child forgets how crucial eating was to her basic survival, she should relax and eating should become a more pleasurable experience.

Food and Attachment

Food is the most essential element in creating attachment. Although most toddlers are capable to a certain degree of feeding themselves, adopted toddlers should not be allowed to do this until parents have established themselves as the primary food provider and caretaker.

When possible, parents should always be the ones who feed their child, no matter how resistant the toddler may be. This may include regressing to the bottle stage; sitting in the parent's lap and eating from the parent's plate; the parent feeding and holding silverware while the child is eating; and discontinuing feeding for a short time while the parent continues to eat if the child refuses to allow the parent to feed him.

Attachment inhibitors could include toddlers eating without their parents' help, being left to eat by themselves even if the parents are in the room with them, denial of food as a punishment, or possibly being forced to eat everything on their plate.

Feeding Your Toddler

Feeding your toddler and making dining a pleasant experience is an integral part of bonding and attachment. Find out as much as possible about your child's current diet, her likes and dislikes as well as any allergies that she may have. Chances are that there are many common foods that your child may never have experienced. She may also like some foods that you cannot imagine any child or even yourself eating.

Callie had to learn to eat vegetables and immediately loved but had never been given juice. We had been told that she liked meat and sweets. She also loves bread but has since decided that she does not care for traditional Russian food such as beets or pickles.

For months I tried to make mashed potatoes to her liking. Every time we ate baked potatoes, I would mash hers. I tried adding dill and sour cream and experimented with different thicknesses with a varying degree of results. Finally one day she sat down with her grandmother and started eating a regular baked potato. Who would have thought?

Taste, texture, presentation, and experience will play an important role in your child's eating habits. Callie was so excited the first time I made a boiled egg, but she was picky about how they were cut. She wants boiled eggs to be cut in half horizontally instead of in vertical quarters. She also would not eat scrambled eggs until I started adding a little butter to the pan.

Your toddler may go through a phase where she wants to eat the same thing for lunch every day, eats only green food, or must have ketchup on everything. These are typical toddler eating patterns. You may have to teach your child decision-making and how to choose what they would like to eat. Experimentation is the key to feeding your new toddler.

Determining Your Toddler's Needs

Older toddlers usually have teeth and can bite easily. They can walk with or without help. Most likely they have learned to drink from a cup and can use a spoon. They can eat bite-size food and will chew before swallowing. These toddlers should be able to enjoy a variety of foods including cereal, bread, milk, juice, yogurt, cookies, soups, stews, sliced fruit, sliced raw or cooked vegetables, meat cut into small pieces, pasta, and many other table foods.

Toddlers who are learning to crawl can pull themselves up, drink from a cup, eat with their fingers, and mash food with their gums. They are probably not ready for adult food but will enjoy foods that can be chewed and swallowed easily. Baby foods such as meat and pasta or chicken and rice will offer more variety, flavor, and textures than puréed or single-flavored foods will.

Young toddlers who can sit without support, roll around, eat from a spoon, and swallow without problems most likely still need a variety of baby foods. These foods could include formula, baby cereal, juice, and a variety of baby food. You may also need to consider single-flavored baby food as a starting point and work your way up to mixed foods.

Feeding Problems

Feeding problems can include upset stomach, allergies, food obsessions, overeating, or refusing to eat. Because feeding and attachment are so closely interwoven, address any feeding concerns with your pediatrician or specialist at the onset of these conditions. Common feeding problems can include the following:

Sensitive Tummies: Once you have been granted custody of your toddler, he will experience many things for the first time. Travel, time change, and a change in caretakers all will affect your toddler. This will include many new foods. Start slowly and play it safe. The introduction of new foods is an upset stomach waiting to happen.

The first night Callie spent with us, we were given kefir for an evening snack and told to give her this for breakfast as well. Mommy decided that when in Russia, do as the Russians do. So no kefir for breakfast since I had meat and potatoes in the fridge. We'd had meat and potatoes all week for breakfast; surely this would be far better than the lumpy, brown, rotten-yogurt-looking stuff.

That was only my first mistake; apple juice for a drink, and more apple juice on the plane were the second and third. What followed was not pretty. Airsickness, carsickness, and motion sickness were my christening as a new mother.

Allergies: Approximately 25 percent of children may have some types of food allergies. Symptoms can include runny nose, asthma, colic, rashes, or crankiness. Many times allergies are inherited, but in most cases this information will be unavailable to adoptive parents. You will have to use caution.

Until you are home, avoid highly allergic foods, especially if you are traveling to complete your adoption. Your child's caretaker should be able to give you information about any known allergies. If your child is drinking milk or milk products, chances are they will not produce an allergic reaction.

Highly allergic foods can include milk or dairy products, eggs, corn, wheat, soy, citrus, peanuts or peanut butter, sugar, chocolate, tomatoes, pork, and shellfish.

Introducing one new food at a time will help identify food allergies. Foods that are least likely to produce an allergic reaction are apples, peaches, pears, broccoli, cauliflower, carrots, sweet potatoes, rice, chicken, salmon, and turkey.

Food Sensitivities: These may include sensitivity to food coloring, preservatives, sugar, and other stimulants. Your child may have limited exposure to any number of these and may experience hyperactivity, overstimulation, crankiness, and irritability. These reactions may mimic the affect of Attention Deficit Disorder and Attention Deficit Hyperactivity Disorder.

Avoid chocolate, beverages that contain caffeine, and foods with red and blue dyes. Juice, cereal, and other snacks can be overloaded with many of these irritants. Good basics are cheese crackers, simple cereals, animal crackers, and other simple low-sugar snack foods. Do not use low-fat products. Use whole milk, if your child is not drinking formula. Include

100% fruit juice, fresh fruits and vegetables and as many all-natural products as possible in your child's diet.

Hoarding and Bingeing: When times get tough, children in orphanages may be fed tea and bread. Children who are malnourished, experience hunger, or have a fear of being hungry may hoard, steal, or binge after adoption.

Children who are malnourished or have been abused by having food withheld are more susceptible to having food-related issues. While some children will eat until they make themselves sick, others may show no interest in food.

Children who have food related issues might have to have their food regulated. It may be necessary to find positive ways to reinforce the fact that food will always be available. It is necessary that your child receive proper diet and nutrition. Parents must determine their child's needs versus their wants.

Sensory Integration: Lack of stimulation and underdeveloped senses can result in tactile and auditory processing problems called sensory integration disorder. This disorder can include problems with auditory processing and hyper- or hyposensitivity to noise, touches, or sight. This sensitivity may manifest as an oral aversion to food, including problems with taste or texture or simply having food in the mouth.

The theory that "when she gets hungry enough, she'll eat" may not apply to children with a sensory integration oral aversion to food. These children must learn to eat. One mother in an adoption group told me that when her child was adopted he was slowly starving himself to death and no one in the orphanage would make him eat. She also told me she once held his mouth closed for forty-five minutes so he would not spit his food out. Ultimately she prevailed.

The degree of seriousness may vary, and many children who have sensory integration issues may happily eat a limited diet. Trying new foods, particularly with different textures, however, can be a problem. Consult your pediatrician at once if you suspect your child's eating problems are more than a dislike of the food she is being given. You may be refereed to an occupational therapist or other specialist.

Chapter 10

Bath Time

Whoever wrote the nursery rhyme "Rub-a-dub-dub, three men in a tub" forgot to mention the real reason they were all in the tub: It takes six hands to give a toddler a bath! One to keep them in the tub, one to hold the washcloth, one to pour the soap and shampoo, one to lather and rinse, one to prevent injury, and one to keep them entertained.

Of course three men equals one Mommy, but Callie's first bath was given to her by her father. I hate to admit this publicly, but I was quite impressed that he had taken it upon himself while I was doing some last-minute shopping. Callie loved the bath, but that's not to say that there haven't been some moments since then!

Memories of Bath Times Past

Each toddler will come with bath experiences, which will vary greatly depending on the age and situation he was in prior to adoption. Adopted toddlers may never have been bathed in a bathtub; their baths may never even have had warm water. And while baths should be pleasant experiences, they may have been just the opposite for your toddler.

It is also quite possible that the only bathing that your child received was a cold shower or from a washbasin with a washcloth. If your child is from Eastern Europe, he may never have been in a bathtub. He may want to stand up in the tub and most likely will not understand the concept of sitting down. You will need to exercise extra caution during this adjustment period. Regardless, never leave your toddler alone, even if he has no problems sitting up.

The shower at our daughter's orphanage was similar to a locker room shower, and one hotel we stayed at had a "shower room." Callie enjoyed baths from day one, but she hated water in her face and eyes. While we were washing her or washing her hair, she would stand up and hold on to the tub rail. I suspect there must have been a similar device at the orphanage.

The Bath-Resistant Toddler

Children who have been abused or neglected may not have been bathed regularly or may be resist touch. During this bath adjustment, they may be terrified of the bath. While bathing a bath-resistant child can be frustrating and emotionally draining, it is actually a good opportunity to strengthen your attachment. He will come to trust that bathing is a pleasant experience.

If your child is bath-resistant, you may have to bathe with him (some people choose to wear swimsuits to do this) or have him in the room with you while you bathe in order to familiarize him with being bathed in or around the tub. It may take a child several months before becoming comfortable with sitting in the tub. Naturally, bath toys can be good enticements.

Bath Essentials

Here are the bath essentials:

- •Bath sponges
- •Bath toys
- •Brush, comb
- •Bubble bath
- •Diaper ointment
- •Diapers, underwear
- •Faucet covers
- •Lotion
- •Nail clippers
- •Nonskid mat
- •Pajamas
- •Shampoo
- •Soap
- •Swivel or Suction Bath Rings
- •Talcum powder
- •Toothbrush, toothpaste
- •Towels, hooded towels
- •Washcloths

Before you start the bath, always check the water temperature. Water that may be the perfect temperature for you may be too hot for your child, especially if you are like my friend who likes her bathwater so hot it turns her skin pink! Water temperature should be warm enough to stay warm for the duration of the bath without causing discomfort.

A nonskid mat will help prevent falls, and faucet covers can help prevent scalding and head injuries. Swivel or suction bath seats or rings should be used only if your child can sit up by herself. Again, never leave your child unattended while in the bath.

You probably would not want or need to purchase a bath seat or ring unless your child is a young toddler or has special needs. There's also a good possibility that you may not be able to use a bath seat. This will depend on your child's comfort level in the tub.

Other bath essentials include washcloths (I like animal-shaped ones) or bath sponges and towels or hooded towels. Use soap and shampoo for babies with sensitive skin until you can determine if your toddler has any allergies. Shampoo should be gentle enough for little eyes, and depending on your child's hair type or length, you may need a no-tangles formula.

Restrict the use of bubble bath to older toddlers. Use sparingly, especially for little girls who can be more susceptible to urinary tract infections.

Of course all children can tell you that baths are no fun without toys, and there are a wide variety to choose from. I prefer ones that can dry easily, and I shy away from bath books or cloth bath toys that need to be washed frequently because they can harbor germs. Callie's favorite bath toys include her bath blocks and a bath baby doll.

Toys should always be developmental and age-appropriate. A toy shelf is a great place to store bath toys. They stay tidy and are usually designed so that the water will drain off the toys.

After you dry off your toddler, he will most likely streak across the house naked (or jump up and down on the bed). If you are fast enough to catch him before this happens, you will be able to add any lotions, powders, or ointments; diaper him or put on underwear; put pajamas on; clip and file fingernails; bush, comb and dry his hair; and brush his teeth. If you have to chase your child thought the house, you will still need to complete the ablutions upon his capture—but then you can have some quiet cuddle time. Reading to your toddler will help him unwind before bedtime.

Chapter 11

Diaper Care and Potty Training

The age of the toddler you are adopting will determine her diapering needs. If your toddler is in diapers, you will have to decide between cloth and disposable diapers. The biggest advantages to using disposable diapers seem to be that they absorb moisture and keep wetness away from baby's skin. They also fit more securely and you can throw them away rather than having to wash them or use a diaper service. One disadvantage is that they do not promote potty training because the child does not feel as much discomfort at having a wet or dirty diaper.

Changing a Diaper

When my husband and I began the adoption process, we had no clue how to change a diaper. For diaper changes, you will need the following:

- Clean diapers
- Diaper cream or petroleum jelly
- Disposable diaper wipes
- A change of clothes if necessary

Now here's how to change a diaper:

1. Remove the dirty diaper and use diaper wipes to clean the baby. For little girls, wipe from the front to the back. This is important to help prevent urinary-tract infections. Little boys have great aim so be sure to drape them with a clean diaper. Throw away the dirty disposable diaper and wipes in an odorless diaper pail.
2. If needed, use diaper rash cream or petroleum jelly as directed by your pediatrician.
3. Put on the new diaper according to the instructions on the diaper package.

Diaper Rash

If your child is coming from an orphanage, he may not have had his diaper changed as frequently as needed and may have developed a nasty case of diaper rash. Get a pediatrician's recommendation on how to treat diaper rash ahead of time. It can be very painful. The following tips can help soothe diaper rash:

- Change the diaper as soon as your toddler soils it. Do not use baby powder.
- If possible, let your toddler go bare-bottomed for a time. The air will help dry out the diaper rash.
- Do not use plastic pants or disposable diapers if possible. They can make diaper rash worse.
- Wash the toddler with soap and water; baby wipes can cause additional irritation.

Circumcision

If you are adopting a boy, he has most likely not been circumcised. If you wish to consider circumcision, you will need to speak to your pediatrician. She can discuss the advantages and disadvantages as well as answer any questions that you may have. She may refer you to a urologist. In most cases, circumcision is considered cosmetic surgery and health insurance usually will not cover the cost of the procedure. Check with your insurance provider.

Potty Training

If your toddler is an internationally adopted child, she may have already started potty training. How a child has been potty trained and at what age will vary by country. Your adoption agency should be able to give you some insight to help you prepare.

Some Eastern European countries begin potty training at twelve months, and adoption agencies may recommend that you bring a potty chair with you when you travel to adopt your child. If your child is between twelve and twenty-four months, skip the potty-chair and just plan on using disposable diapers or disposable training pants. Most likely she is not truly potty trained but was put on the potty to go at certain times of the day. If she misses her window of opportunity, she will have an accident. Most likely, she will not have the communication skills or understand the concept of going when she needs to.

Plan on using an average of seven to ten diapers a day. You should be able to purchase diapers in most places; however, you probably want to take enough to last you several days. You may also be able to buy a potty-chair in your host country.

You may need to take a potty-chair with you when you travel to adopt older toddlers who would be more secure in their potty training. You may be able to get away with taking a potty seat rather than a potty-chair. A potty seat fits on top of a toilet seat and is much smaller than a whole chair. This may or may not work. Ask your adoption agency if a potty seat would be an acceptable substitute for a potty-chair. Using a potty seat may be a problem in places where toilets are more like latrines. When we were in Russia, everywhere we went had a different type of toilet. Flushing was an adventure because the handles were in different places on different toilets. All the toilets were shaped a little differently, and they did not really have seats as we know them. We could not have used a potty seat even if we needed to.

If the toddler you are adopting is closer to thirty-six months, you may also be able to skip taking a potty-chair with you on your trip. You would however need to take disposable training pants or cotton training pants. Disposable training pants can be pulled up and down just like regular underwear but will help prevent accidents. Make sure they come apart at the side. If they don't, it can be really messy if your child has diarrhea. This is especially important when changes of diet and travel are occurring or if your child has to sleep with you. Also take either a few pairs of cotton training pants or regular children's underwear in case your child is used to wearing it and refuses to wear the disposable diapers.

We opted to take a potty seat with us because it was much smaller than a potty-chair, but we did not use it. Our daughter, who was three-and-a-half at the time of her adoption, was still living in the baby house when we adopted her. In group settings, children often have little flexibility in their schedules and are expected to go to the bathroom to comply with their regimented schedule. To be safe, we kept her in disposable training pants during the three days she was with us prior to reaching home. She did not have many accidents and used the toilet or *gorshok* that we had been given by our facilitators.

The *gorshok,* which was actually a version of a Russian potty-chair, still rides with us in the car in case of emergencies. We have been grateful to have it. It looks like a little plastic-covered casserole dish; when I saw them in the orphanage, I thought they were used to store children's belongings.

Children who are in the process of potty training or who are potty trained may regress when life-altering changes are made. This occurs in children who aren't adopted as well as adopted ones. Even if your child is 100 percent potty trained and under the age of four, I would consider disposable training pants a necessity while you are traveling. Kos, who was adopted at two years old, was already potty-trained. However, at the age of three, about a year after he was adopted, he was just beginning to reacquaint himself with potty training. Karina, adopted at eleven months, had no interest in potty training until she was four.

Our daughter used a potty-chair at the orphanage, but she did not get to decide when she went to the bathroom. She especially enjoyed exercising her newfound independence. She quickly learned that she received an immediate response to her expressing a need to relieve herself. We would sometimes have to take her to the bathroom four or five times during dinner. She enjoyed the cause and effect: She decides that "I am bored so I want to get up, maybe play in the sink while washing my hands...I can sit with Aunt Kathy when I come back, I am scared and want to leave, etc."

Fortunately most of the novelty has worn off, but she will still try on occasion if she is bored. We have to determine if she is faking or really needs to go. Just be flexible—accidents will happen.

Chapter 12

The Medicine Cabinet

As with any medication, consult your physician before giving medication to your children. In your initial consultation with your pediatrician, he or she will give you recommendations on which medication to use as well as when and how to use it. Always follow your physician's instructions on administering medication. Read the warnings and patient advisory information. This material warns you of any possible allergic reactions to medication or other possible side effects. It could save your child's life.

All medications should have childproof caps and be kept out of children's reach. Many medications are made to be child friendly. Medications that are in the form of lollipops or other candy, freezer pops, or juice bottles contain a special hazard to children who can not differentiate between regular treats and medication. These and other medications should always be stored in a locked medicine cabinet.

A well-stocked medicine cabinet should contain the following items. (This list is meant to be used as a glossary of available products as well as their uses. I am not, however, advocating or endorsing any specific product to be used in place of professional medical advice.)

Adhesive bandages—Sterile bandages designed to cover and protect wounds.

Allergy medication—Used to treat common indoor and outdoor allergy symptoms, including stuffy nose, runny nose, sneezing, itchy, watery eyes, coughing, etc.

Antibiotic ointment: A first-aid antibiotic used to help prevent infection in minor cuts, scrapes, and burns.

Antihistamine: Used to treat allergic reactions.

Charcoal: Used to neutralize the ingestion of poison. Use only as directed by a physician or the Poison Control Center.

Cold medication: Used for the treatment of common colds, allergies, and upper respiratory infections. Available in a variety of flavors with a variety of products to treat different symptoms, including stuffy nose, runny nose, sneezing, itchy, watery eyes, coughing, etc.

Cotton balls: Good for a variety of uses including cleaning cracks and crevices as well as cuts and scrapes.

Cotton swabs: Ideal for a multitude of uses. If used to clean ears, stroke swab gently around the outer surface of the ear without entering the ear canal.

Digital thermometer (or other thermometer): For oral, rectal, or underarm use; fast and easy to read temperature.

Fever reduction medication and pain reliever: Helps reduce fever and provide relief of minor aches and pains due to colds, flu, sore throat, headache, and toothache.

Hydrocortisone cream: For the temporary relief of itching due to minor skin irritations, inflammations and rashes due to eczema, insect bites, poison ivy, soaps, detergents, and more. For external use only.

Hydrogen peroxide: A topical antiseptic used to clean wounds and help prevent infection.

Medicine dropper: Used to administer any liquid medicine by mouth, as recommended by your child's doctor.

Nasal aspirator: Provides gentle suction to remove excess mucus when your child has a stuffy nose. Helps make breathing easier.

Oral electrolyte maintenance solution: Quickly restores fluid and minerals lost from diarrhea and vomiting. Used to prevent dehydration.

Oral pain reliever: Relieves teething pain, and provides temporary relief of sore gums due to teething.

Petroleum jelly: Helps prevent diaper rash, soothes chapped lips and skin, moisturizes, and lubricates.

Poison reduction medication: To be used after ingestion of a poisonous substance to induce vomiting. (Contact Poison Control before administering.)

Rubbing alcohol or alcohol swabs: An antiseptic skin cleanser. Can be used for cleaning thermometers, tweezers, etc.

Saline nasal spray: Nonmedicated moisturizing nose drops for relief of dry, irritated, stuffy noses due to colds, allergies, dry air (humidity), or air pollution.

Sunscreen: Used to protect skin against the sun's ultraviolet rays, which cause sunburns as well as skin cancer. Fair-skinned internationally adopted children from Eastern Europe may be particularly susceptible to sunburn, as they may have spent little time outdoors and aren't used to the different climate. Use a sun block with an SPF 20 or more and limit the amount of time the child spends in direct sun.

Toddler ice pack: A small ice pack designed to fit a few ice cubes or a freezer ball. Sometimes animal shaped. Used more for moral support for minor bumps or falls than to treat real injuries.

Vaporizing cold medicine: An external medication used through inhalation to provide temporary relief of nasal congestion and coughing due to colds. Also provides relief as a decongestant and cough suppressant.

Chapter 13

The Pediatrician

Selecting a Pediatrician

Choosing a pediatrician is an important step in your child's health-care plan. A pediatrician will be your child's primary physician. If your child has special needs, your pediatrician may have to coordinate a health-care plan or refer you to a specialist, depending on your child's needs and your insurance plan.

Because a physician should examine your child soon after his arrival, you should select a pediatrician in advance. The best place to get a physician referral is from parents of young children. Your adoption agency or social worker may know of a physician in the area who has adopted patients. Ask members of any adoption group or other adoptive families in your area whom they recommend. Your obstetrician/gynecologist or primary care physician could also give you physician referrals.

In our case, I was referred to a popular children's clinic. The administrator I spoke to was very insistent that I attend an orientation meeting for new clients instead of scheduling a private consultation. I suspected and, after asking enough questions, confirmed that this orientation meeting was for expectant parents and covered what to expect at the hospital before and after birth and infant care—what to expect during the first few weeks. This was completely inappropriate for a parent who is adopting a fifteen-month-old toddler with specific health concerns and questions, not to mention extremely insensitive to the infertility issues of adoptive parents. Furthermore, since I had been clear in my explanation that we would be first-time parents who were adopting a toddler from Eastern Europe, this attitude made me question their ideas and opinions on adoption.

The pediatrician I initially called to set up a consultation never called me back. When I called a second time to schedule a consultation, I was referred to another doctor in this practice. She did not return my call on a timely basis (within two or three days) either. I concluded that since my phone calls were not being returned now; they probably would not be returned when I had other medical questions or emergencies.

In the interim, a friend referred me to another pediatrician. I had called her to ask for a pediatric referral. She pointed out that the two practices I had originally been referred to were a twenty- to thirty-minute drive from my home. She felt that even though I make that drive regularly, it might be farther than I would want to drive with a sick child.

The pediatrician my friend Betsy suggested was great. His office was less than ten minutes from my house. He seemed genuinely interested in and supportive of adoption. His parents had visited several orphanages in Eastern Europe, and I assumed that he had a working knowledge of the conditions these children live in. He also showed a willingness to receive and research medical information pertinent to adoption issues, and he understood what it would mean to have an incomplete medical history and did not consider it a hindrance.

Here are a few things to consider when choosing a pediatrician:

1. What are the office hours?
2. What are the after-hours and weekend policies and procedures?

3. Are there other adopted patients? Are there other patients who are internationally adopted or have the same ethnic background?
4. Does this physician meet your insurance requirements?
5. How long does it take you to drive from your home to the doctor's office?
6. Does the pediatrician have a positive attitude about adoption? Does he or she appear willing to learn more about special needs of adopted children?
7. What is your general impression when you look around the office? Is it neat and clean?
8. Is the staff friendly, courteous, and helpful?

The Consultation

Before your consultation with the pediatrician, you should make a list of the questions that you have. This will help you conduct your interview and remember the important questions. The pediatrician should be willing to review your medical information, be able to discuss your child's current medical condition if applicable, and be able to refer you to specialists as necessary. She should be up-to-date on the health issues of internationally adopted children or be willing to seek additional information as recommended by the American Academy of Pediatrics or International Adoption Specialist. She should also be willing to review your child's videotape.

If you have birth children or if it has been many years since you have had a young child in your home, it may be necessary to use a different pediatrician. You might now need one who may be more knowledgeable in adoption issues or one who specializes. For example: I found out that one of the pediatricians I was referred to worked with many children with asthma and was frequently out of the office teaching and conducting asthma-related medical business.

Most pediatricians do not charge for consultations. Out of courtesy, be conscious of the amount of time you spend with the doctor. Make sure your questions have been answered to your satisfaction but do not get off track. This consultation should help you determine whether you would trust this person to oversee your child's health care not teach you child-care basics.

The First Examination

Medical examinations by a pediatrician soon after you reach home are necessary to get an accurate assessment of your child's current medical condition. At this time the pediatrician may recommend your child see a dentist or pediatric dentist, have an eye exam, or hearing and speech evaluation. He will also address any immediate medical concerns.

See the American Academy of Pediatrics, Provisional Section on Adoption, for medical information on adoption and foster care at *www.aap.org/sections/adoption.* The provisional includes an introduction to the health-care needs of adopted children, the importance of screening tests for internationally adopted children, immunization, and infectious diseases. Some of the most common infectious diseases include hepatitis A, B, C, and D; intestinal parasites such as giardia; tuberculosis; HIV; and syphilis.

Immunizations

Because immunization records may be inaccurate, most immunizations should be repeated. Even though you may have received documentation indicating immunization records, there is no assurance that your child actually received the immunization or that the medication was given accurately and had not expired. Testing for antibodies will enable your pediatrician to determine if antibodies are low or nonexistent and whether it is necessary to re-immunize.

Failure to re-immunize and/or failure to check for antigens/antibodies from past immunizations should be a serious red flag and is considered essential for your child's health and safety.

When Do I Call My Pediatrician?

As a new parent, trying to determine whether your toddler is sick (or sick enough) and whether you should contact the pediatrician can be tricky. When you selected a pediatrician, you should have been given information to help determine if your child is sick, if he needs immediate medical assistance, the policies regarding calls received after-hours, and what temperature fever indicates a problem. As with any medical recommendations, always follow the advice of your physician. Reasons to call the pediatrician or other health-care resources may include:

1. Your child looks and acts sick.
2. Your child has a fever of 103 degrees or higher. (Follow *your* pediatrician's recommendation. A lower fever and lethargic toddler could also warrant a call to the pediatrician. When in doubt, make the call.)
3. Your child has a rapidly rising temperature.
4. Your child will not eat or drink.
5. Your child has dry skin, a dry sticky mouth, no tears, or infrequent wetting. These may be signs of dehydration.
6. Your child vomits after falling or other injury.
7. You are worried about your child's illness.
8. Your child is very sleepy, restless, fussy, or shows other changes in behavior.
9. Your child has had several episodes of diarrhea and/or vomiting.
10. Your child experiences severe diarrhea while on medication.
11. There is blood or mucus in the diarrhea.

12. Your child has difficulty breathing
13. Your child has a cold that is worsening or accompanied by a fever.
14. Your child is drooling and cannot swallow.
15. You suspect your child may have ingested chemicals, plants, pills, or other hazardous material.

For common illnesses such as a cold or upset tummy, it may not be necessary to consult your pediatrician. Helping ease your toddler's discomfort will be high on your priority list. (The first cold is the worst.) Giving toddlers plenty of fluids and making them rest will help make them feel better.

Make sure your child drinks plenty of fluids. Too much juice can cause diarrhea. Watch for dehydration. Feed your toddler according to his normal schedule. You may need to feed smaller portions and more easily digestible foods such as crackers, mashed potatoes, chicken noodle soup, or toast.

If your toddler has a cold, you may need to use a humidifier in his room to help moisten his breathing passages and sore throat. It may be necessary to prop your child upright in bed to help him breathe more comfortably. A bulb syringe can help clear a toddler's nose.

Watch for signs of increased discomfort or an increase or addition of a fever. It is also important never to give a child aspirin. Use an aspirin substitute. Your pediatrician can recommend one.

Changing Pediatricians

Selecting a pediatrician in advance is kind of like shopping for a new dress. It might look good on the rack, but you can't tell how it fits until you try it on. Once your pediatrician actually exams your child, you may decide that you do not wish him to continue as your child's pediatrician.

I "fired" the pediatrician I had selected in advance when the TB specialist he referred me to had to use a medical instrument to remove my daughter's ear wax buildup. I am sure that I had seen the pediatrician check her ears, and this should have been a standard part of any thorough medical exam.

Apparently the pediatrician decided that he was smarter than (or had never read) the information that I had given him containing recommendations by the American Academy of Pediatrics for internationally adopted children. I discussed this with him during our initial consultation and hand-delivered a copy of the report to his office immediately before we traveled.

Instead he refused to test her stool and urine. (Yes, I actually brought samples to the office.) He also refused to run an antibody/antigen test to make sure she had received her immunizations and that what she had received had done its job. He even misquoted the article concerning re-immunization and stated that it was not necessary.

At the time we had been home less than forty-eight hours. I was too tired to argue with him and could not tell him where this information had come from when I tried to question his decision.

This was the same pediatrician who in my interview was very positive about adopted children. He also appeared willing to learn more about their health needs. He also had some knowledge of children in orphanages, as his parents had visited several. I thought this doctor should have been up-to-date on current medical information.

It is amazing that he actually tested for tuberculosis. Luckily he did and after a positive TB test, we were referred to a specialist for children's infectious diseases. She was up-to-date on medical concerns for internationally adopted children and knew what should be done. She did everything the pediatrician failed to do.

The stool sample showed that Callie tested positive for giardia and had to be treated. The specialist ran blood tests and even checked her for chickenpox scars. She did not think Callie had been exposed to chickenpox or had immunity. The antibody test showed that she had. Failing to re-immunize or to conduct diagnostic testing could unknowingly leave your child vulnerable to such illness.

Fortunately we went to see her the first week we were home. She also referred me to another wonderful pediatrician. Always have a backup plan. Educate yourself on adoption-related health concerns, and if in doubt, get a second opinion.

Chapter 14

Medical Considerations for Adopted Children

Medical reports for our children are sometimes the largest hurdle that a parent has to face when considering adoption. The reports can be incomplete or nonexistent, misrepresented, incorrectly translated, inaccurate, and, in rare cases, falsified. They may need more follow-up, a physician's review of the available information, and further research on medical conditions, insurance coverage, and medical resources within your community.

This added work may even add delays to your adoption process. That being said, you should never allow yourself to be rushed by an agency to make a decision. It is also considered unethical for an agency to enforce a hold deadline while waiting for medial information.

You should be given ample time to review a child's medical info, have it evaluated by medical personnel, and decide whether you would like to pursue the adoption.

Physicians Who Evaluate Medical Information

More serious or chronic medical conditions should have been diagnosed before the child is available for adoption. The younger a child, the harder it is to get an accurate diagnosis of medical conditions. One advantage in adopting toddlers over infants is that I believe you can get a more accurate diagnosis of a child's medical condition, developmental level, general personality, and well-being.

There are physicians who are experienced in and available to evaluate medical information and videotapes of children. If your adoption agency did not recommend having a physician review your medical information and videotape of your child (if this information is available), be sure to have this done for any other children that you consider for adoption. The information that is disclosed to families will vary by country.

Physicians who review medical information of internationally adopted children are experienced in evaluating children who were premature, had low birth weight, or have developmental delays as a result of being institutionalized from birth. If the evaluation results in a negative prognosis or a possible medical condition, consider a second opinion. One specialist recommended this course of action to us.

If two physicians independently arrive at the same or similar conclusions, that helps eliminate the likelihood of misdiagnosed medical conditions. However, a physician's review of videotapes or medical data can never replace a physical examination. Some medical conditions have no physical symptoms. Without a physical examination, it is possible for a physician to misdiagnosis a medical condition or suspect one that the child does not actually have.

Doctors are more likely to err on the side of caution. If a physician suspects a child has fetal alcohol syndrome or fetal alcohol affect, he or she should be able to give you specific details and an explanation of the physical characteristics that look suspect. The doctor has an obligation to the family who may have already, at least on some level, bonded with this child to help them understand the risk factors and what they should consider acceptable risks.

An Independent Medical Exam

In some countries it is now possible to have a physician visit your child in their home or orphanage and perform a medical evaluation. This is usually an independent, Western-trained physician who is available for hire. This practice occurs mostly in Eastern Europe and Russia and is becoming more and more common. The examination is costly, running anywhere from $500 to $1,000. You may or may not have to be present for the exam.

More and more orphanages are allowing conference calls between physicians and other personnel to answer questions regarding a child's health. When possible, adoption agencies can help coordinate conference calls and physician exams for you. They must seek permission from the orphanage director, who may or may not allow it.

Medical Records

Medical history for an adopted child may be inaccurate, incomplete, or nonexistent. Be aggressive; insist on obtaining as much medical information as possible about your child's current medical condition, birth parents, and family history prior to placement. This will allow you time to research any known medical conditions and make post-placement arrangements for treatment. Once the adoption is complete, it may be impossible to obtain any additional information about your child's birth family or medical history.

Inaccurate medical information is seen more frequently in internationally adopted children. One of the most common complaints among adoptive parents is a misdiagnosed medical condition. This can occur for many different reasons, including an inaccurate medical diagnosis made in order to release a healthy child for adoption or, in rare cases, an inaccurate diagnosis to allow a child with a more serious medical problem to be adopted. Most commonly, medical terminology is used differently in other countries or a broad-based, seemingly meaningless term may be used to describe a variety of medical issues that may not be discovered until after the child has arrived home and been examined by a physician.

Incomplete medical information may occur due to poor record keeping, a frequent change in caregivers or social workers, or even purposeful omission of medical information with the intent to hide a child's background information or history of sexual or physical abuse.

It is also possible that medical information may not actually be missing because there was in fact no medical care available. Children who are abandoned may not have any birth parent information. Children who are in orphanages may be located in remote regions where it is difficult to get information in and out, the orphanage director may be unwilling to cooperate, or there may be laws that set limitations on the type and amount of information that is disclosed.

Medical treatment in foreign countries is not the same as in the United States—nor is medical training. This can often lead to undiagnosed or misdiagnosed medical conditions. We were told that her birth mother being ill at twenty-nine weeks caused our daughter's cleft. By week 29 of a pregnancy, this part of the baby is already formed or, in her case, not formed. The truth is that she has Van Der Woode's syndrome, an inherited genetic dominant trait that can cause a cleft lip and or cleft palate and lip pits.

Our daughter's records were handwritten on assorted pieces of paper. We were given copies and had them translated by the facilitating agency. There were still gaps, however; what we were given was a summary not a literal translation. Have papers like this translated by a third party, preferably someone who is a physician or at least familiar with medical terminology in your child's native country.

In the back of my Blue Cross/Blue Shield physician listings booklet, I found a section of physicians who are bilingual. Believe it or not, I found a Russian-speaking pediatrician in the next city.

Children in Orphanages

It is not uncommon for children who are living in orphanages or other less-than-desirable living conditions to have lice, scabies, vitamin deficiencies, anemia, impetigo, lactose intolerance, malnutrition, internal parasites, rickets, tooth decay, or other medical conditions that may need immediate attention. You may need to consider taking a variety of medications with you when you travel to get your child. (See Chapter 18, "Packing for Your Trip.")

Medical conditions may include sensory deprivation and integration, sensitivity to light, attention deficit disorders, and attachment disorders. The children may also have been premature, had low birth weight, or prenatal exposure to drugs, nicotine, and alcohol. Ear infections and hearing loss as a result of infection are also not uncommon in orphanage babies who are left unattended with their bottles. The quality of the water, a lack of fluoride, and poor hygiene can lead to tooth decay and gum disease. Children with lactose intolerance may show symptoms as infants with this condition becoming more prevalent as the child gets older. Asian, African American, Native American, and Latino children are more likely to develop this condition

Chronic medical disorders should have been disclosed prior to your decision to adopt your child. These may include hepatitis B or C, tuberculosis, and congenital heart disease. Congenital disorders could include cleft palate and cleft lip. Neurodevelopmental disorders include Down syndrome, fetal alcohol syndrome, fetal alcohol effect, and cerebral palsy. HIV and AIDS are on the increase in developing countries.

I have not gone into detail with this, as much of this information is already available through other adoption and medical-related media. You may also find reference material in the Resource section in the back of this book.

Love Marks and Mongolian Spots

Two commonly mistaken birthmarks are known as love marks and Mongolian spots. Love marks seen in children adopted from China are small scars, usually on the stomach or chest. These scars resemble a small burn but are actually made with acupuncture needles or a lighted medicinal plant. This ancient practice is a way of letting the child know that their birth parents loved them and should be considered an important part of their heritage.

Mongolian spots are spots that look like bruises but are in fact birthmarks common in children of Asian or Indian decent as well as black children. These black-and-blue marks are usually on the lower back and buttocks and are sometimes mistaken for bruises. As the child gets older, these marks usually fade but do not completely disappear.

Bransen, who is adopted from Vietnam, has them and even though I knew what Mongolian spots were, had his mother not shown me, I would not have recognized them when I saw them. They looked like ink stains, and his mother told me that a nurse at the doctor's office had mistaken them for that.

If your child has Mongolian spots or love marks, inform and educate caregivers, babysitters, teachers, or medical personnel ahead of time. This may save you and them from possible embarrassment if they inadvertently see them and think the worst.

Medical Support and Available Resources

If you are adopting a toddler with physical, cognitive, developmental, or speech and language problems you should find out what resources are available in your area. Your adoption agency, social worker, or home study coordinator may be able refer you to state and federally mandated programs, including rehabilitation and subsidies. Adoption agencies that frequently deal with the department of social services may be able to refer you to more specialized services. Other resources include your pediatrician, social services, local children's hospitals, specialized support groups, adoption support groups, international/ethnic organizations, the Internet, your insurance company, the school system, or other children's agencies.

As a precaution, consider finding a family counselor or child therapist in case you need help during your adjustment period or if you have bonding issues or concerns.

If your child is an older toddler and speaks a different language, it may be necessary to secure an interpreter prior to placement. Our daughter was three when we adopted her. My cousin's wife is Russian and was able to serve as an interpreter. Another couple who adopted an older child had an interpreter visit regularly so they were able to communicate better with their daughter while she learned English. This could be potentially life-saving in case of illness or an emergency.

Callie was born with a cleft lip and palate. I was able to contact our pediatrician and get several referrals including a plastic surgeon, children's hospital, and a genetics center. Each referral was able to give me more referrals. While researching Callie's medical condition, I was able to find resource information on the Internet from the Cleft Palate Foundation, various support groups, and a variety of specialists.

We were able to assess her current medical condition, learn what medical procedures might be necessary, and her prognosis. We were also able to see before-and-after pictures of children with similar medical conditions, get cost estimates, and check insurance coverage. We also were also able to select two cleft teams who would evaluate our daughter upon her arrival.

If your child has a known medical problem, you have an obligation to yourself and your child to make informed decisions concerning her medical treatment. You must be mentally and physically prepared and financially able to provide the best treatment possible. Know your options.

Developmental Assessment, Early Intervention Programs, and Speech Therapy

An examination to determine your child's developmental level is essential for adopted children. If your child has been in an orphanage, he will probably be developmentally behind, at the rate of approximately one month behind for every three to four months in the orphanage.

This should help qualify most adopted children for some type of services, whether it is speech, occupational, or physical therapy. If your child is under age three, contact a local early intervention program that can assess your child's need for special education or related services.

Once your child's developmental level has been determined, consider enrolling him in activities that are at his developmental level rather than at his actual age. This may involve advocating for the rights of your child.

Sometimes programs are subject to individual interpretation of the laws or rules regarding eligibility. Occasionally there is prejudice against internationally adopted children. It may be necessary to contact your local congressional representative, senator, or other government official to ensure that your child receives the benefits that he is entitled to.

It pays to know the actual terms of eligibility for state and federal programs. The Individuals with Disabilities Education Act states, "All children with disabilities must be provided free and appropriate education." Programs for children over three are usually overseen by the school district, and they are required to test in the child's native language. Do not wait until your child understands English before testing for eligibility for services.

The trick is getting an appointment before your child loses his native language and does not have enough of his adopted one. Most developmental tests for children who are toddler and preschool age are language based and should be conducted by a speech and language pathologist not a psychologist.

If a child is developmentally delayed, he may be considered learning disabled based on test scores, even if he is simply a year behind. A developmental delay, regardless of the reason, is considered a disability. However, he may only participate in age-appropriate programs, not developmentally appropriate public programs, including preschool and kindergarten.

The reason for this is simple: money. State or federally funded programs receive their money on a per-student basis, and the criterion is chronological age. I strongly disagree with this practice. Adopted children should be eligible for developmentally appropriate, not age-appropriate, therapy and education.

Most public early intervention programs and child development programs are either fully or partially funded by state or federal funds. There is often a delay in getting appointments, completing the assessments, and beginning services. Much of this is due to the meeting the eligibility requirements to begin a program and completing the paperwork. If this sounds vaguely familiar, that's because it is. Apparently these offices work with the same sense of urgency that many offices we are already familiar with do when processing adoption paperwork.

If your child is eligible for services, an Individual Education Plan (IEP) will be developed, and it will be necessary to research your child's disability and know your rights. At times, it may be necessary to enlist the aid of an advocacy group. What you consider to be appropriate services for your child may not coincide with your school district's idea of appropriate. For example, placing a speech-delayed child in a classroom with hearing-impaired children or with children who are learning disabled because they are a year behind age-appropriate peers.

Because our daughter had a cleft lip/palate, she was eligible to receive speech therapy. During this assessment, she had a developmental assessment and was required to have a speech and hearing assessment as well as a vision check. Speech therapy is a federally mandated program. All children over the age of three are eligible for free speech services.

I was told that because of Callie's cleft, she was immediately eligible to begin speech therapy; normally children who are learning English as a second language are required to wait two years before they can enter a program. Many school systems offer classes in English as a second language. These classes usually start at age four, and many children in these classes speak Spanish as their first language.

Plan ahead. I waited until after our daughter had recovered from her palate repair surgery to set the initial appointment for an evaluation to begin speech therapy. The appointment was set for six weeks after I called. In total, it took us four months before our daughter could begin to receive speech therapy. Of course as my frustration begin to increase, I was told if I did not like it to call my congressional representative. This comment was unnecessary and unwarranted because I had not even begun to get angry at that point.

Since this program is offered through the school program, Callie only received three months of therapy before school was out for the year. She was able to attend a six-week summer program. In total, the first year home, she only received four and a half months of therapy.

It took us four months to get an appointment to see a developmental pediatrician. First, no one responded to our pediatrician's multiple referrals; then they sent us a package of papers to fill out, their office moved, it was Christmas, and finally, they lost our paperwork (luckily I had keep copies). I had no idea that after taking four months to get an appointment, it would take three months to get the assessment.

Misdiagnosis of Medical Conditions

It may be impossible to diagnose some medical conditions before your child arrives and is examined by the pediatrician. Most experts recommend that a pediatrician examine your child within twenty-four to forty-eight hours of arrival. This examination should be a basic "everything looks okay; let's schedule a more thorough examination in a few weeks after your child gets more adjusted" appointment.

The good news is that with proper diet, nutrition, and medical care, many children have a remarkable growth and development spurt within their first year home. However, medical conditions for internationally adopted children may sometimes be overlooked or misdiagnosed because their conditions may be less common in the United States. Diseases and illnesses that are common overseas may be very rare or even nonexistent in the United States. Adopted children could also be at higher risk for contracting an illness that children born in the United States either have some natural immunities from or were immunized for.

If in doubt of your child's medical diagnosis, or if medication is not working, be persistent. You are your child's health-care advocate. Use your adoption networking resources. Chances are you are not the first person who has experienced this.

Chapter 15

Child-care, Preschool, and Babysitters

One of the most controversial issues of all time is child-care. While religion and politics are always two hotly contested subjects, you will soon learn that there are two more: being a stay-at-home mom versus being a mom who works outside the home and whether to circumcise your adopted son.

Whether you have the luxury of staying at home or must make sacrifices to stay at home with your child, or you choose to work or must continue working, you will still need to use an occasional babysitter and be responsible for having an educational plan for your child. Neither side gets its much-deserved respect.

I can still remember a former employer contemptuously spitting out the words, "She doesn't have a clue. The biggest decision she will make today is what is for dinner." While this attitude can be found in the work place, there is also often resentment from childless coworkers who can't appreciate the need for time off to care for a sick child. Although it certainly does not hold true for everyone, I have found that many employees secretly long to be a stay-at-home parent, and many of them are in denial.

Most stay-at-home moms get little respect. Even those who should know what staying at home entails (like friends, the husbands and fathers) are often clueless. I was responsible for purchases in excess of $10 million and regularly worked 60-plus-hour weeks. As a stay-home mom, I work in excess of 100 hours a week and do not get to go home at the end of the day and rest and unwind. I work at home from morning to night. The job is never-ending and far from glamorous. When people ask what I do all day, I tell them I eat bonbons and watch soap operas. It doesn't matter if they believe me or not, it's what they think regardless.

Babysitters

On occasion, everyone needs time away from their children, whether it is a night out with friends, a quiet evening alone with your spouse, or time to run errands. Your needs will vary and will be determined by your toddler's age, adjustment, and development.

The best place to find a babysitter is through friends or personal references. Among the best sitters I've found are our friends' children. We always told them that we would have children when theirs were old enough to baby-sit, and that has worked out perfectly. Of course, they do have to vie with Grandma and Grandpa who cherish the opportunity to spend quality time with their granddaughter. It is definitely advantageous to have at least one set of grandparents living in the same area.

If using a service or a sitter you are unfamiliar with, always meet the person in advance and check references. Your child's needs will determine what age sitter would be appropriate. The more needs your child has, the more experienced a sitter you need. Sitters should never be under age thirteen, and many cities have child-care/babysitter training available for teens. Your sitter should be responsible enough to act accordingly in a minor emergency.

Ask your sitter to arrive early so you can show her or him around the home, give instructions, answer questions, and review potential problems. Show the sitter where first-aid kits and flashlights are located and give emergency contact numbers. Is there a neighbor he can contact if necessary? Leave emergency numbers, cell phone numbers, beeper numbers, and the location and phone number where you will be by the phone.

Tell the sitter when you will return home and, when applicable, be sure her parents approve the time she will be home. If you are late, inform both the sitter and his parents.

Child-care

Most people would like to enjoy the best of both worlds; that is, working a limited amount of hours doing a job they enjoy, being able to afford a reduction in hours, and having their child in a part-time program with other children. For those who wish to pursue this, it may take some creative thinking by both you and your employer.

You may wish to choose in-home daycare or use a daycare center. Your best resources come from other parents. Ask friends, coworkers, your doctor's office, your social worker, or your adoption agency for suggestions. Child-care sources could include your church, child development centers, newspaper ads, or other child-care agencies, including those that specialize in nannies or au pairs.

If you choose to have in-home care, you may have more decision-making freedom regarding how your child spends her time, what she is fed, the rules regarding discipline, and so on. In-home daycare is often more expensive than a daycare center. When choosing in-home care, use a child-care service or an agency to help you find the best-qualified person to suit your needs.

Consider your options and then screen, select, and check references on sitters or programs that you may be more interested in. Before you interview a sitter or visit a daycare center, decide what is important to you and prepare a list of questions. When trying to determine which program is best for you, consider the following:

- Is the daycare licensed or registered per state requirements? How long has it been in operation?
- What are the caregiver's qualifications? Do they require a degree in child development or other related subjects? How long has your child's caretaker/teacher been employed?
- What are the admissions requirements? Are they reasonable? What other requirements must be met before enrolling your child (such as immunizations, potty training, etc.)?
- Is the location convenient, and do the hours of operation suit your needs? Do they charge late fees? What are the costs, and are they reasonable for the services provided? What is the pickup and drop-off policy?
- What is the child to caregiver ratio? (State requirements will vary.) What is the age of children in attendance, and are the children grouped by age?
- Do they have an open-door policy? Do they encourage parent participation or observation? Is the staff accessible to parents?
- What are polices involving sick children, accidents, and so on? Do caretakers have training in CPR or first aid? What is the policy regarding emergencies? Do they report all accidents to parents?
- Are the premises neat and clean? Are safety features or other child-proofing devices visible? What is the condition of the toys, playground and so?
- Are classrooms dark, small, or sparsely furnished, or are they roomy and cheerful with artwork exhibited? Do children in attendance appear happy or complacent? Do you get good "vibes" or are you hearing warning bells? Do you think your child would enjoy spending time here?

- Do they offer preschool-equivalent educational services, field trips or other activities, or do children have continuous supervised free play?
- How are birthday parties or other holidays celebrated?
- Do children have naps or quiet time? What are the sleeping arrangements? Are there separate areas for sleeping, play, food preparation, and toilet needs? Does the facility provide snacks or meals, and if so are they nutritious?
- Do they provide references? The best are those you get by word-of-mouth from someone you know, not those provided by the center.
- How do they handle child conflict or discipline?
- What is the policy regarding (voluntarily or involuntarily) dropping the program?

Preschool

I relish the fact that my children attend school. In theory, that means I have "me" time. To bad it is often interrupted with doctor's appointments, shopping, running errands, or house cleaning. I do accomplish a significant amount of "work" during this time; after all, I don't have time for rest and relaxation—I'm a mom now.

While my free time is important to me, how my children spend their time is equally important. Once a month I receive an itinerary of school activities, which include subjects discussed in class, colors, and numbers, as well as physical activities, music time, and chapel. I enjoy receiving these because I can ask specific questions about their day or know what they missed if they were not at school.

Preschool is the time for children to learn social skills such as sharing, taking turns, and cooperation. There are a variety of preschool programs available. Some programs will focus more on academic achievements. Many will be provided by faith-based organizations, while others are strictly private institutions or provided through the public school system.

While most of the considerations for daycare are the same when choosing a preschool, they should also include the following:

- Does the school focus on an educational curriculum or more on social interaction? Which is more appropriate for your child?
- How long is the class? How many days a week?
- Do they offer extended stay?
- Do they have parent and teacher conferences? How often?
- What type of activities do they do? Arts, crafts, books, music, outdoor play, field trips, etc.?
- What are the program's goals or expectations for your child?
- Do they provide school supplies or do you?

Special Considerations for Adopted Children

Choosing the right daycare or preschool program is never an easy process, especially if you have many options. However, as a parent of an adopted toddler, you should be aware of some special considerations. Most important, is your toddler ready to attend daycare or preschool, or have a regular babysitter?

Separation Anxiety and the Fear of Being Left

Most likely, your toddler's classroom will consist of one room with one teacher and a lot of children. If that sounds familiar to you, just think how familiar it will feel to her. She may have a fear of being left or experience separation anxiety. While it can be traumatic, it is not uncommon for toddlers—adopted or not.

Your toddler may be terrified, thinking she is being abandoned or "returned." She may find any unfamiliar area upsetting. This may be the result of previous disruptions, insecure or newly formed attachment, inconsistent care, or grief.

If there is a high employee turnover rate at the daycare center, you may need to reconsider. Consistency is very important for adopted children. How much personal attention will your toddler receive? There should be enough caretakers to hold, cuddle, or comfort her.

Give her time to adjust to her new schedule. You may choose to start slowly, while others jump right in. She may need reassurance that you will be returning to get her. Never sneak out when your child is not looking; this can create trust issues. Be prepared, it is harder on Mommy than on your child.

On the other hand, some toddlers may be totally unaffected by attending daycare or preschool. For a recently adopted toddler, or a toddler who is secure in his attachment, this may be an easy transition, and he may easily accept this as part of his new routine.

Indifference for toddlers who have been home for some time should be looked at more closely to ensure bonding and attachment are progressing. Sometimes toddlers may become attached to caregivers and may not want to leave or experience confusion when it is time to go home. This is a situation you need to watch closely; you may need to rethink your child-care options.

The Classroom and Curriculum

Prepare in advance. We drove by Callie's preschool quite often before she started attending. She had previously attended Mommy's Day Out, and each time we told her this was her new school that she would be going to in the fall. When the first day of school arrived, she was very excited and well prepared.

Learning social skills has been Callie's biggest obstacle. In an orphanage, the squeaky wheel gets the grease, and it is not uncommon for workers to have favorites. Callie was one of these, and the only girl in her age group. She did not understand that she was not the teacher's assistant but was supposed to sit with the rest of the children. She also learned it pays to be cute and is a master of diversionary techniques when she is being scolded.

Preschools usually focus on an educational curriculum or social interaction. You need to decide which is more appropriate for your child: learning cooperation, taking turns, sharing, having increased social interaction in a noncompetitive environment, or focusing on academics, catching up to same-age peers, learning letters or numbers? (These elements do overlap to some extent.)

Programs should stimulate development in a nonstressful environment while not being overly demanding or too advanced. Your child should be comfortable in his classroom setting and not overwhelmed, stressed, or lost.

Consider the length of time in class versus at home. We opted to hold Callie back a year in school, starting 3K not 4K as was age-appropriate. Maturity level, length of time in an orphanage, and significant cleft-related speech delays all played a role in this decision. We also did not feel that we wanted her to spend more time away from home than at home, considering that she was three at the time of her adoption. Even though we have only had mild bonding and attachment issues, we felt it was more important to continue strengthening her adjustment to family life.

Special-Needs Children

How does the school feel about children who have not learned to speak, are learning English as a second language, or are developmentally delayed? What are the rules involving conduct or other nonharmful inappropriate behavior? Do they appear positive or apprehensive about adoption? Do they ask inappropriate adoption-related questions? What questions were you asked? Are they genuinely interested in your child or are they interested in sensationalism?

You should discuss in detail any concerns or special needs that your child has. The more information that you can provide (excluding personal specifics such as the child was abandoned at a maternity hospital, etc.), the better understanding your daycare provider may have.

Find out if there are other adopted children or if they have experience with dealing with adopted children. If your child has special needs, are they able to accommodate him? What are the procedures regarding special dietary needs or administering medication?

Have a Backup Plan

Once your child arrives home, you may decide that your predetermined child-care plan does not suit your child's needs. In some cases, children need more time with their new families before beginning a child-care program; their medical needs may be greater than anticipated; or a parent may decide to change his or her work schedule. Having a backup plan will help should the need arise.

Chapter 16

Losing a Referral

Losing a referral is a possibility that many adoption professionals do not like to discuss, but I would be remiss if I did not include a segment on losing a referral. Unfortunately, it is also a topic that I am too familiar with. We lost our first referral from Russia after nine months and were defrauded by a birth mother in the United States who was convicted of felony grand theft by deception.

As with most adoption statistics, there are no records of how many adoption attempts actually result in the loss of a referral. I do know, from an informal survey conducted during an adoption playgroup, that international adoption has a higher success rate than infant domestic adoption.

The type of adoption and country you are adopting in will be an important factor in assessing the risk factors and should be a consideration when making that decision. Reasons for failure to complete an adoption can vary. Countries can issue moratoriums and open and close their borders to adoption at will. Family members may come forward and claim the child, or there could be other circumstances in which the child is discovered not to be a legal orphan. One example would be the child's father visiting him in the orphanage. In Russia, Russian families take precedence over American families, and a Russian family could adopt the child you are planning to adopt—even though you have accepted his referral.

Another example would be awarding custody of a child in the foster care system to his birth parents who may contest the adoption. The Bureau of Citizenship and Immigration Services can refuse to issue a visa if they are not satisfied that the paperwork is legitimate. It is also possible that you may have to decide to decline the referral for health concerns or other reasons after meeting the child.

Some adoption agencies will tell you that they rarely have an adoption fall through, and that may be the case for that particular agency. Other agencies are up-front with clients and prepare them for the possibility, and some agencies never discuss losing a referral with clients. Either way, it is never easy for families who lose a child for any reason during the adoption process.

Fraud

Adoption fraud is a "cruel and unusual" crime. Unfortunately there is too little protection for parents who are often subject to birth parents' demands or adoption agencies with which they may have invested thousand of dollars.

Good record keeping and documenting conversations during the process will help in the event an adoption falls through. Know what your contracts mean and get everything in writing, especially pertaining to the services provided and the policy regarding a failed adoption. Are monies prorated or do you get full credit toward another adoption? What are you entitled to if you decide to change agencies?

Too often, there is no recourse for families who may be emotionally devastated or financially unable to pursue appropriate legal action. Tougher laws and use of existing law must be made accessible to victims of adoption fraud or abuse. It may take creativity to make existing laws applicable for adoption fraud.

No one has the right to purposely defraud or misrepresent themselves or their agency during the adoption process. This includes negligence, lack of product knowledge (not understanding adoption procedure, laws or risk), inexperience, or purposeful criminal intent.

If you or someone you know has been victimized by an agency or individual, report it to the proper authorities. These agencies include the Better Business Bureau, the state licensing specialist, the state bar (for attorneys), your local congressional offices, the consulate or embassy, or various adoption-related entities.

If you are not sure where to begin, start networking, using the Internet, or contacting various advocate organizations such as the Adoption Guide, *www.theadoptionguide.com* or the Inter-Country Adoption Registry, *www.adoptachild.org/ICAR/index.asp*.

Grief

Losing a child during the adoption process is similar to having a death in the family. Months before we lost Anastasia, we had completed a nursery, bought a minivan, and had baby showers. Many of our friends, family, and coworkers knew her by name. We had months of attachment before we lost her referral. Adoptive parents, like birth parents, do not wait until the child is born or an adoption is complete to form attachments. Adoptive parent attachment is frequently misunderstood and underappreciated by those who have not personally experienced it.

Adoption support groups may not be able to provide support either unless another member has experienced adoption loss. Adoptive parents can be very critical of adoptive families who choose to tell their story in a public forum, even when fraud or other ethical issues are involved. Because they cannot relate to the family's experience, they may see it as simply another negative adoption story.

The loss of our first referral delayed preattachment to Callie to a certain extent, and it was several months after accepting Callie's referral before I could take Anastasia's picture out of my wallet. There is also a lingering doubt of never knowing what really happened and what has become of this child. The name we had chosen for Anastasia had to be put away, never to be used again. Occasionally I find something that reminds me of her and I feel the loss. I suspect it is something I will carry with me forever.

In my opinion, many agencies use the bicycle method—if you fall off, they put you right back on. Too often, families are not given time to grieve. Mourn appropriately. How much time you may need will vary. Don't rush yourself, allow anyone to rush you, or hurry into making decisions. It is important to take the time to consider all your options, even ones that may result in financial loss.

Mary Lib Mooney, founder of the Adoption Guide, lost the referral of a child during the Russian adoption process. She recommends "grief counseling for families who have experienced an adoption loss." On occasion, adoptive parents or prospective adoptive parents experience depression as a result of losing a referral.

Moving Forward

The information in this chapter might have made you uncomfortable. The intent was not to be the bearer of bad news but to make you aware of potential problems that we were not prepared for. While we could never have been fully prepared for losing a referral, it would have helped to know that while it may only occur in a small percentage of adoptions, it does happen regularly. In our case, we did not find out until after the fact. It was, however, within days of joining an adoption-networking list.

As devastating as loss of a referral can be, most families who experience it will tell you that they went on to successfully adopt the child or children that were supposed to be theirs after all. It may have taken a lot of strength and determination, but eventually the paths they took led them to their children.

By the time we lost Anastasia, it was almost a relief to have closure. Had it not been for her, we probably would not have found Callie. If you experience an adoption loss, get up, dust yourself off, take the time you need to grieve, explore your options, seek help if necessary, and decide what is best for your family.

Adoption is a great lesson in faith and patience—the latter being something I frequently do not have enough of. Perhaps the hardest part of adoption is the waiting. But if you have faith to sustain you, then you will come to realize that ultimately whatever child is supposed to be yours will be.

Chapter 17

International Adoption

In 1989, the total number of immigrant visas issued to orphans coming to the United States was 8,102. In 1999, this total had more than doubled to 16,396.

In 2000, of the 18,120 children adopted, 40 percent (7,239) were toddlers, one to four years of age. Infants under one year of age accounted for 48 percent of those adopted. Of the 8,784 children under one year of age who were adopted, the majority were six months old or older due to a variety of reasons including birth country requirements. With an average age of nine months, these babies are just on the brink of "toddlerdom."

According to the U.S. Department of State's Office of Children's Issues, for fiscal year 2001, there were 18,699 immigrant visas issued to orphans coming to the United States. This is a 13.8 percent increase from 1999.

Interestingly, international adoption increased less than 1 percent between 2000 and 2001. This would suggest that perhaps the number of families adopting internationally has finally leveled off, or perhaps some families chose to wait until the Hope for Children Act (adoption tax credit) went into effect in January 2001. Many families who were ineligible for the $5,000 adoption tax credit in 2000 are eligible for the new $10,000 tax credit if they have a gross adjusted income of $150,000 or less.

For 2001, the top ten countries of adoption by U.S. citizens are as follows:

Country	# of Adoptions
China	4,690
Russia	4,279
South Korea	1,770
Guatemala	1,609
Ukraine	1,246
Romania	782
Vietnam	737
Kazakhstan	672
India	543
Cambodia	407

Approximately 90 percent of all international adoptions by U.S. citizens take place in these ten countries. Of this 90 percent, 37 percent of the children are adopted from Eastern Europe or former members of the Soviet Union, 40 percent from Asia, 9 percent from Guatemala, and 3 percent from India.

No significant increases or decreases were seen in adoptions from China, Russia, South Korea, Guatemala, Vietnam, or Cambodia. Both the Ukraine and Kazakhstan had significant increases in international adoptions. Ukraine had an 89 percent increase in international adoptions, preceded by a 104 percent increase in the year 2000. While there were 1,246 children adopted from the Ukraine in 2001, only 323 were adopted in 1999. Kazakhstan had a 68 percent increase in adoption.

Much of this increase is due to changes in Russian adoption law. Many people who had initially planned or were considering a Russian adoption in 2000 switched to the Ukraine, Kazakhstan, or elsewhere as rumors regarding shutdowns, delays, and ever-changing laws were and still are common. Switching countries is not uncommon as countries regularly change adoption regulations or open and close their borders to adoption.

Romania had a significant decrease in adoptions in 2001. Both Romania and Moldova had moratoriums on international adoption for most of 2001. Significant decreases in international adoptions should be expected in both Vietnam and Cambodia for 2002 as both countries have placed international adoptions on hold.

Traveling Abroad

Before traveling to complete an international adoption, families should review Consular Information Sheets and Travel Warnings. This information is available from the State Department's Bureau of Consular Affairs. It can be found on the Internet at *http://travel.state.gov* or by calling (888) 407-4747 ([317] 472-2325 after-hours or overseas).

Consular information sheets are available for every country in the world. This information may include a description of the country, entrance and exit requirements, HIV testing requirements, areas of instability, aviation safety and air travel, traffic safety and road conditions, medical facilities, crime information, currency exchange, customs regulations, adoption, drug penalties, and registration at U.S. embassy locations.

You may also find listings for services and other pertinent information for citizens who are abroad. These listings include the numbers for emergency services; where to go for help with lost or stolen passports, financial assistance, arrest and incarceration; lists of doctors and hospitals; and links to U.S. embassies and consulate Web sites.

As a safety precaution, always look up consulate and embassy locations before traveling overseas. Be sure to carry their addresses and phone numbers with you at all times.

Immunizations

After you begin the adoption process, you may find that a variety of immunizations for illnesses not commonly found in the United States are recommended. The Center for Disease Control (CDC) has recommendations for international travelers by country or region at *www.cdc.org.*

Most likely, you will need hepatitis A and B and DPT (diphtheria, tetanus and pertussis). You may also need a measles booster, polio vaccination, flu shot, or other immunizations or health precautions, depending upon where you will be traveling.

Insurance should cover immunizations, but you may want to check with your health-care provider in advance. If your insurance company is denying coverage, have your physician's office call them and forward the CDC's recommendations and risk of exposure. It may be necessary to appeal if insurance coverage has been denied. It may also be possible to have immunizations done at the health department. They are usually less expensive.

If you are required to have HIV testing prior to an adoption, it may be significantly less expensive at the health department. In South Carolina, it is $10 at the health department and more than $100 at a physician's office.

Customs

When you enter another country, you may need to declare the cash and valuables that you are taking in with you. Flight attendants should have customs forms and should be able to answer questions that you may have. If you make a customs declaration, make sure you have your paperwork stamped as you enter customs and do not lose it because you'll need it when you exit the country.

You should declare all money that you are carrying with you; depending on the amount, it may be necessary for you and your spouse or companion to split the money. It is possible that the customs agent may want to count your money. You should consider this when "hiding" money in multiple locations. We were unprepared for this event and had to scramble to locate the rest of the money while the agent held our other money. Later that evening we discovered that we were $100 short. I'll give you two guesses where we suspect it went.

The U.S. Embassy

During your adoption journey, you will be required to visit a U.S. embassy. You must take your child to an interview so that he can be issued a visa to enter the United States. Embassies are closed on U.S. holidays and on the holidays of the host country.

Prior to your exit interview, your child must have had a medical exam either at an American medical clinic or by a physician approved by the embassy. You must take a color visa photo of your child with you to your appointment. You will be able to get this done when your child is photographed for his passport.

You may arrive at the embassy to find that a protest is taking place, and it is not uncommon to encounter long lines, usually of locals applying for visas. U.S. citizens do not have to wait in line but are allowed in the embassy for their appointments.

You will be required to go through a security checkpoint and will encounter armed guards. Your facilitator may or may not be able to enter with you. He or she should have organized your paperwork for you and explained what you need and what to expect.

Interviews consist of a brief review of the paperwork. Paperwork errors or delays do happen and could result in your having to stay a few extra days while they are resolved. These interviews are usually conducted in the morning, and visas are completed and can be picked up in the afternoon. However, this policy has been streamlined at some embassies so that only one visit is required and the visa is issued while you wait. There will be many other adoptive families at the embassy, and you will find that some of these families will be on your return flight home.

When you receive your child's visa you will be given a sealed package of papers that should be packed in your carryon luggage where you can easily reach it. You will need it when you enter the United States. You will also need documentation including your child's visa when you exit your host country.

Travel Insurance

Travel insurance is available for U.S. citizens traveling overseas. You may wish to consider this option before traveling outside of your home country or country of residence. Many professionals in the travel industry recommend travel insurance. Considering the total cost of an adoption, travel insurance is relatively inexpensive at around $100. The longer you expect to be out of the country, the greater the need to consider travel insurance.

The primary function of this insurance is to help offset the cost of emergency medical evacuations and the repatriation of mortal remains. Coverage may include incidental medical expenses, an emergency family reunion, and accidental death or dismemberment. It may also include necessary political evacuation or expulsion from the host country, trip interruption in case of an emergency, or lost baggage. International assistance services may include medical assistance while you are traveling and other general travel assistance.

Adoption Travel

You may get the call to travel with little advance notice, perhaps only one to two weeks. Most agencies will put you "on call." When it starts getting close to the time to travel, they will tell you that you may expect a travel date soon.

Until you have a confirmed travel date, do not make any arrangements that could result in a cancellation fee or that are nonrefundable. Tickets should be flexible because return dates could change. Some airlines and hotels offer adoption rates; always ask.

When making travel arrangements, consider travel agencies that have experience working with adoptive families. They will have experience making arrangements with minimal notice and will know who offers the best deal at the time. Your agency should be able to give you recommendations and will frequently make part or all of the travel arrangements for you.

Length of Stay

For international adoptions, your travel options will vary by adoption agencies and will be determined by your child's birth country. A few countries allow someone to escort your child home. If this option is available, it will be discussed with you when making your adoption plan.

You may be required to make one, two, or possibly even three trips to complete your adoption. Some countries may require you to spend a certain amount of time with your child before the adoption hearing, while others may allow you just a brief visit.

Most likely, you will have to attend a court proceeding to complete the adoption and either be granted custody of your child at that time or return a second time to bring her home. If a second trip is required, you may meet your child on the first trip and complete the adoption on the second trip.

Your host country will determine the length of your trip. It is not uncommon for many business offices to be closed during holidays, and waiting periods are usually counted as business days. Weekend days are usually not counted toward ten-day waits. Vacations can postpone court dates and the completion of other business. It seems that when someone is on vacation, which frequently lasts several weeks at a time, there is no one to fill in for the vacationing party.

All rules regarding adoption procedures, including the number of trips required and the amount of time you are required to visit your child or remain in the country, are subject to change at any time. Some countries have better records than others regarding policy changes; these changes rarely occur without some warning. Rumors regarding adoption policy and changes in procedures are rampant. Consider the source and rely on your agency to address these rumors as necessary.

During extended stays, try to do as much sightseeing as possible and absorb your child's culture. Visit museums, churches, or cathedrals; sample local cuisine; attend the circus or ballet; explore tourist areas or other famous landmarks or memorials. You may also be able to help out at the orphanage and spend a lot of quality time with your child.

Air Travel

Depending on the airline you choose, you may be able to fly coach/economy, business, or first class. Some international airlines may offer business class seating equivalent to what we consider first class, and they are often no more expensive than a coach seat on another airline. On return flights that are not full, flight attendants will sometimes upgrade adoptive families.

Consider traveling as direct a route as possible. This will help minimize your travel time and decrease the risk of missing connecting flights. Once you have been granted custody of your child, you will most likely be anxious to return home. Don't add additional travel or sightseeing to your trip after you have been granted custody for a variety of reasons, including possible health concerns or adding additional confusion and time to adjust for your child.

When flying on an airline that is not American owned or operated, investigate their smoking policy. This is especially important if you or someone in your party has asthma or smoke allergies. Smoke may be more prevalent in economy or coach seating.

Make sure that the person booking your tickets understands that you will be traveling with a small child. You can request bulkhead seating, which offers more legroom and sometimes a foldout baby bed. You should request a child's meal in advance for your toddler. When traveling with a small child, it may be necessary to enlist the help of the airline between connecting flights. These arrangements should be made in advance.

Many airlines offer adoption rates. However, it is not uncommon for travel agents or airline personnel to be unaware of these discounts. If you know that an airline does offer adoption fares, it may be necessary to speak to a supervisor or someone who is more knowledgeable in discounting rates. If you travel on two separate trips, the adoption rate may only be applicable for the second trip, during which you are bringing your child home. If you have been quoted an outrageously priced ticket, look around before committing; most likely you will be able to find a better rate.

Children over two years of age must have their own seats in an aircraft regardless of their size. While it is not required, it is recommended by the Federal Aviation Administration (FAA) that all children under forty pounds ride in a FAA-approved child safety restraint system. Children under forty pounds will not fit in an airline seat properly. It may be logistically impossible to carry a child seat with you, and most likely it will be impossible to keep a toddler buckled in any type seat for any extended period. If your child is not buckled in his seat and you experience turbulence, he should be buckled in immediately.

One alternative to taking a car seat is the Baby B'Air flight vest. It secures to your lap belt, may be used in flight, and is considered much safer than holding a child in your arms. It is not allowed during takeoffs, landings, or taxiing in the United States. Check with your airline; some now provide child safety restraint systems. Families who travel with an FAA-approved child safety restraint may receive discounted tickets for their children.

Takeoffs and landings may be painful to little ears. One way to relieve air pressure is to give a child something to drink during this time. Another alternative is Mack's earplugs. They are available in a child size for children under age six. Earplugs are small wax plugs that are placed over the ear opening as a cover. They do not go inside the ear itself.

Some adults may also benefit from earplugs or "Ear Planes." Ear Planes help relieve ear pain, clogging or popping, and regulate air pressure. If you have frequent sinus pain or pressure, you may also benefit from taking sinus medication prior to air travel.

Train Travel

Depending on where you are traveling to and airline availability, you may end up arriving at your final destination by train. In most cases, you will need to purchase an entire cabin, and a facilitator or interpreter will travel with you.

Trains are slow moving and cabins are small. When we were in Russia, we met a family who had spent fifteen hours on a train for what would have been an hour-and-a-half flight. This had been their only option as all flights to the area had been booked.

Car Travel

On occasion, it may be necessary to travel by car for several hours if your child is located in a more rural area. This can be an adventure in itself. Most likely there will be no rest areas or bathroom facilities. (Welcome to the great outdoors!) Roads may be in poor condition or unpaved, people may drive on the opposite side of the road than you are used to, and weather conditions may be less than ideal.

Even within city limits, there may not be street lines. In Russia there were potholes large enough to swallow an entire car, and all cars driving in the same direction drove side–by-side, filling the width of the street. When cars came from the opposite direction, drivers jostled for position behind each other to make way for approaching traffic.

If you have ever ridden in a cab in New York City, you may recognize a similar style of driving. Be warned, there is a good possibility that your driver may make a New York cab driver look like Grandma on her way to church on Sunday.

People in many other countries do not use car seats for children. Most likely, you will not be able to use a car seat in a vehicle if you take one with you. Your child may have never ridden in a car and may experience motion sickness or even be terrified. Chances are he has not ridden on a train or airplane either.

Networking: Know the Area

Several factors will help determine the ease of adoption travel. Use an experienced adoption agency that has a good team of facilitators, and network with families who have traveled before you. There are a number of Internet resource groups for adoptive parents who have already completed or are in the process of completing an adoption.

You should be able to find families who have adopted from the same region or country that you are adopting from. Try to find families who have traveled most recently so you can obtain the most current information. You may want to know about the following subjects:

- Appropriate dress
- Availability of products: toiletries, baby items, bottled water, etc.
- Cash, credit cards, American dollar conversion
- Court procedures
- Customs
- Embassy visit
- Emergency contact or an independent or non-agency-affiliated interpreter
- General safety concerns
- Hotel and homestay options
- Internet access
- Medical care

- N
  p
- C
- C
- I
-]
-
-

Fan
option
Wher
accon
with
had v
within ten minutes,

After a fifteen-minute break, we had a meeting with our facilitator. asked why we could not stay at either of two hotels that I knew by name. They were surprised and impressed that I knew the hotels.

We suspected that our facilitators knew the owner and that they were actually trying to save us money. We later found out that it was conveniently located to our facilitators' home, but they did not have any problem moving us. We offered to pay the week's fee to be moved. (It was between $6 and $8 a day and included meals.)

Fortunately I had talked to several other families who had recently been to the same city and knew our options. Moving literally saved our trip. We were taken to the popular regional hotel in the heart of the city. Located on the waterfront, it had a beautiful view and was surrounded by several restaurants, outdoor cafés, parks, and a port where cruise ships docked. We also knew several area restaurants by name. Our staff genuinely appreciated that we had taken the time to learn about their city in advance and that I had learned a limited amount of Russian.

Chapter 18

Packing for Your Trip

Purses, Handbags, and Luggage

Many people have legitimate concerns that their luggage will arrive and arrive undamaged. If you must purchase new luggage for your trip, consider luggage on wheels. Seasoned travelers will often recommend hard-sided luggage over soft-sided. Cloth luggage may easily be torn, and hard sides prevent thieves from cutting it open and stealing your things. Luggage locks are all similar, and most can be opened easily. Whichever type you choose, consider replacing the locks.

You may notice in airports overseas that people wrap their luggage in what appears to be clear plastic wrap. This is another way to help deter would-be thieves. I am not sure if ii is worth the hassle, as it may also help draw attention to your baggage and is not allowed for air travel within the States. I recommend the use of basic black or dark-colored luggage. Use discretion—no red, tapestry, or animal-print luggage. Although it may take longer to find at baggage claim, you want your luggage to blend.

Duffel bags are also commonly used in Europe, and some are fairly large. You may want to consider the weight of your luggage prior to packing. Many large suitcases are very difficult to carry when filled to capacity, but they should be light enough to carry as needed. You may have to carry your luggage for some distance without the use of wheels in unpaved parking lots, while climbing stairs, and so on. Weight restrictions and number of bags varies by airline. You will be charged additional fees for overweight luggage or for going over baggage requirements.

If you are taking a large quantity of orphanage donations, it may be necessary to have a letter of verification from your adoption agency. Be sure to notify whoever is picking you up from the airport in case additional arrangements must be made. It may be possible to have baggage fees for orphanage donations waived, and you should inquire about this when making your travel arrangements.

If you are planning on returning home with fewer pieces of luggage than you arrived with, consider purchasing inexpensive luggage either at a discount store or from a resale shop. Luggage stores may have slightly damaged pieces that they would donate for this purpose. Extra room in suitcases left after giving away gifts or donations makes room for souvenirs.

No traveler wants to arrive at her destination only to find that her luggage has been lost or stolen. To avoid serious problems, hand-carry all adoption documents, including visas and passports. (Carry extra copies in your checked baggage as well.) All necessary prescription medication should be included in your carryon luggage.

If there is room in your carryon bag, you may want to try to include one change of clothing per family member, a couple of your gift items, and assorted toiletries. You should also split your belongings between your checked bags. At the very least, each person should have a set of clothes in each bag. You may also split gift items and donations between bags.

When possible, carry identification, cash, and credit cards on you, perhaps in a money belt, a belt bag, or fanny pack. Any time you are in a crowded area be aware of potential pickpockets. This includes groups of young children.

Carry a small handbag or a wallet on a string that can be worn across your chest, shoulder to hip, under your coat or jacket. No one can come up behind you and grab your bag, and it will rest on your hip where you can easily reach in or hold it.

Since September 11, airline policy has changed regarding carryon bags, and you should check for each airline's requirements. Most will only allow one carryon bag per person. This may be especially important if you have several connecting flights and will be flying on different airlines.

A handbag or pocketbook may count as one piece of carryon luggage. If you purchased a seat for your child, then you are also allowed to bring an equal allocation of carryon luggage for her. There are no restrictions regarding a child's carryon luggage. While a stroller or a diaper bag would most likely be counted as one piece of carryon luggage, a child safety seat would not.

Don't pack nail files, scissors, razors, or pocketknives in carryon luggage. If possible, wear a bra that does not have underwire. If you have a clothing item that has caused problems (I own a pair of boots that has previously set off security alarms), do not wear it while traveling.

Health Care and Toiletries

In many parts of the world, personal need items such as soap or diapers are readily available, while other items such as baby wipes or disposable training pants will not be. Be prepared and plan ahead; you may have little or no choice in selecting a brand name.

You may need to pack some or all of the following:

- •Adult wipes
- •Antibacterial hand soap
- •Bath soap
- •Cordless curling iron
- •Cotton balls
- •Cotton swabs

- Hair dryer
- Nail clippers
- Personal hygiene items
- Petroleum jelly
- Scissors
- Shower shoes
- Sunscreen
- Thermometer
- Tissues
- Toilet paper
- Toothbrush/toothpaste
- Towels and washcloths
- Tweezers

For your child, pack the following:

- Baby shampoo
- Baby thermometer
- Baby wipes
- Bath toys
- Bulb aspirator
- Diaper bag
- Diaper rash medication
- Diapers/disposable training pants
- disposable changing pads
- Hooded towels
- Lotion
- Pacifiers
- Plastic training pants
- Potty chair
- Sunscreen
- Teether or teething ring

Medications

You should take all prescription medication in the original bottles along with copies of your prescription or the patient advisory information sheets, which usually include the doctor's name, pharmacy information, and the use for the medication. I prefer taking the patient advisory because it provides information concerning the use of the medication as well as doctor and pharmacy information.

Most likely, you will need to consult your physician for prescriptions for medication that you can take with you such as a broad-based antibiotic to treat infection, prescription-strength antibiotic ointment, hydrocortisone, medication for the treatment of scabies, and a tongue depressor for use at your child's embassy medical exam.

When you consult with and select a pediatrician for your toddler, she will give you her recommendations for any medications and dosages for your child. You may need to obtain a prescription for an antibiotic for your child. Size information is frequently incorrect, and you could run the risk of giving your child an incorrect dosage. A note of caution: Do not use this prescription medication for your child without first consulting a physician (one at the orphanage, the embassy, or an independent physician).

It is sometimes suggested to give young children cough, cold, or allergy medication to help them rest or sleep while traveling. However, this could have the opposite effect and cause hyperactivity or increased activity in young children. Most medications for children contain dye, and your child has probably not been exposed to this previously. There is a small risk of an allergic reaction to any medication. This is not something you want to occur at 30,000 feet.

If you have an overactive respiratory system, asthmatic cough, or asthma (even if it is very mild), include an asthma inhaler on your packing list. Air quality and pollution may be bad. Buildings may be old and have "old building" (dust/mold) smells. Fortunately I had heard this and took my inhaler, which I rarely use. I had to use it every day while we were in Russia and continued to use it regularly for two weeks after we returned home.

Take a basic first-aid kit with you. You will also need to take many non-prescription medications to supplement your first-aid kit. Here are a few ideas:

- Anti-diarrhea medication
- Aspirin and/or aspirin substitute (*Never* give young children aspirin.)
- Assorted adhesive bandages
- Allergy medication
- Cough and cold medicine
- Earwax softener (Most likely, your child will have significant buildup.)
- Lice-killing shampoo
- Lotion for sensitive skin (including eczema or dermatitis)
- Medication dispenser (medicine dropper, spoons, or syringe)
- Oral rehydration liquid or powder
- Rubbing alcohol or hydrogen peroxide (both available in swab form)
- Saline nose drops
- Sinus medication
- Upset stomach, heartburn, or indigestion medication

Food to Take Along

Traveling abroad and trying new cuisine will be a whole new dining experience. This includes reading the menu, ordering, paying, tipping, proper etiquette, and cultural protocol. You may be served what you consider breakfast foods for lunch or dinner and vice versa. Because it may not be something that you are used to eating, it may not always agree with you, and you may find that you like the food considerably or dislike it.

My husband can attest to the fact that salted dried fish is not better with beer than peanuts, and our Russian peers were genuinely disappointed in his distaste for it. We had an assortment of meat and potatoes everyday for breakfast, lunch, and dinner. The day I was served fish for breakfast, I drew the line.

Appetizers were called salads and the menu was not grouped by types of food but by price. The concept of how the meat was prepared was foreign to our host, whose explanation of an entrée was not how it was prepared but what it was: meat (beef), pork, chicken, or fish.

Most of your personal food needs should be minimal, but most likely you will want to bring a few essentials, favorites, or snacks along with you for you and your toddler.

You may need to consider travel time and the food that will be available for your toddler during travel. Other than toddler food and snacks, you may need an assortment of silverware, dinnerware, sippy cups, and bibs (consider disposable ones) for your child. You may consider bringing plastic silverware and antibacterial dish soap.

Food for Your Toddler

Plan on continuing your child's current diet as much as possible until you return home. Travel, a new environment, and food sensitivity can all play a role in your child's reaction to new foods. When I was told my child had never had juice before, I should have heeded that warning. Instead we gave her a host of new foods, and not all of them agreed with her. If your toddler is older and able to eat many table foods, play it safe, start slow and bland.

Soy formula is frequently recommended, and powdered varieties are easier to carry with you. If you will be using formula, you will need bottles, assorted nipples, and possibly a measuring cup.

Baby food is usually packaged in glass jars and can be quite heavy. You may want to bring a few jars with you, but most likely you can do without them or purchase what you need once you arrive and assess your toddler's dietary needs.

Rice cereal is a good starter food and will most likely be similar in substance to some foods your child is accustomed to eating. You may have to play with the amount of water or milk that is added. If your child refuses to eat, try making it a different thickness. Callie loves baby cereal but will only eat it if it is very thick.

Popular kid snacks include cheddar crackers, individual-serving cereal boxes, cookies, and toddler food products. Avoid caffeine, chocolate, and foods or juice heavy in sugar, preservatives, or dyes. All of these can cause hyperactivity in children, and there is a good chance that your child has never been exposed to any of them.

Food for You

If you have special dietary restrictions, you may consider taking an assortment of your approved list of foods. Sugar substitute and coffee creamer may not be available. If you are a coffee or tea drinker, you may want to take your drink of choice along with you as well as a hot pot.

If you have a favorite food, it should be on your must-take list. If you have comfort foods that you eat when you are tired, sick, or feeling blue, you most likely will want to pack these as well. (Sorry, ice cream can't go in a suitcase.) Consider taking peanut butter, instant or canned soup, or small containers of canned fruit. You cannot take fresh fruit into another country, and it may or may not be readily available there.

My favorites included applesauce, which saved me the day that we had a stomach virus. Ketchup, a necessity that I did not take enough of, was available but did not taste the same. I found that pretzels and cheese crackers pack better than some chips or crackers (it may depend upon the container), and I wish that I had taken more chocolate-covered peanuts. Cereal/fruit bars did not travel well.

Don't Drink the Water

The single most important dietary rule is do not drink the water! Use bottled water only. Local water supplies may be contaminated with parasites or other waterborne illnesses that locals are either immune to or have adjusted to. Intestinal parasites can cause severe cramping, diarrhea, nausea, dehydration, and weight loss.

Besides not drinking the water, do not use ice, ice products like frozen drinks, or brush your teeth with the tap water. Use caution not to swallow any water while swimming or bathing. Do not wash fresh fruits or vegetables in local water. All fruits and vegetables should be peeled before eaten. That means that salads are off-limits.

Most likely, bottled water will be readily available, and you should not have to take more than a bottle or two with you. Some people opt to bring water filtration systems with them, but you may find that the cost and added inconvenience is not worth the weight. Inexpensive water filters may only be partially effective anyway. In Russia, a standard bottle of water was around 12 rubles (about 35 cents), and we had no problems finding soft drinks.

Miscellaneous

In addition to clothing, toiletries, and food, there are many other items that you may want to consider taking with you on your travels. Space and weight will determine how and what you ultimately decide to take. Buy what you need upon arrival when possible.

Paper Products and Stationery

You may want to record the adoption process in a journal so you have a history of events. If you choose to do this, take your journal with you when you travel so that you can write about your adoption experiences while they are fresh in your mind. There is a good possibility that after you get home, you will not have time to do this.

Another great idea is to take a notebook with consulate information, emergency contact numbers, and any questions that you may have or to write down information that you receive about your child. Attach removable temporary adhesive notes to documents that you may need to help you find them and remember what they are.

We took blank stationery and asked that orphanage workers write notes, information, and/or stories about our child. We were thrilled to receive six personal letters about our daughter.

Cash or Charge

All cash should be crisp, clean, new bills if possible. If not, try to get bills in the best condition possible. Cash that is old and worn may not be accepted. In most countries, it is technically illegal to pay for goods or services in any currency other than that of the host country, but U.S. dollars may be preferred. Your facilitator will advise you when, how, and in what currency to pay.

Take an assortment of denominations, but the bulk of them will probably need to be $100 bills. You will need some smaller bills for miscellaneous expenses such as tipping and for use while traveling in the States. Also, when traveling abroad, it is not uncommon for vendors who wish to be paid in U.S. dollars not to have change in U.S. dollars.

You will need to research whether you can use credit cards or traveler's checks. This will vary by city, region, and country. Usually only very large cities are equipped to handle traveler's checks. You should also inquire about conversion fees for purchases made in a foreign currency.

Notify your credit card company that you will be traveling abroad. If your credit card company sees charges that are made overseas, they may call your home to verify the transactions. Because you will not be at home to do this, your charge privileges may be suspended.

Calling Long Distance

Your travel destination will predetermine your ability to use calling cards, phone cards, a cell phone, or computer equipment. In many cases, your local long distance carrier will be able to provide this service. When researching your phone options, make sure you document your conversation, including your contact spoke and the rate they quoted. This will help in case there are any problems when you receive your phone bill.

We found that it was actually cheaper to call direct from our hotel, bill it to our room, and pay cash than it would have been to use our calling card, call collect, or use various other options. Cell phones, which can be used for international phone calls, are becoming more popular and may be a viable option.

Documents and Other Valuables

Most valuables, including wedding and engagement rings and other fine jewelry, should be left at home. Play it safe and simple with jewelry; take one or two pairs of inexpensive, basic earrings.

Take copies of adoption documents as well as passports and visas. Keep them separate from the originals. This may include giving your facilitator copies or putting copies in a hotel safe.

Batteries, Cameras, and Converters

Make sure to pack your camera and videorecorder, as well as an ample supply of film or batteries, which may be hard if not impossible to find if you run out. Don't forget backup batteries for any toys you may take for your child.

You may need a converter for a battery charger, and most likely, you will need one for hair dryers or various other appliances. Electrical voltage will vary by country. In many places, including Russia and much of Europe, the electrical current is much higher than in the United States and will destroy anything you plug in without a converter.

When we arrived at our hotel in the region, I noticed that none of the appliances or lamps were plugged in. This was the case in Moscow as well. I was told that it was to prevent damage during possible power surges. Use caution when using converters. Beware of sockets that look worn. Never try to repair them.

Laptop and Internet Use

Unless you take your laptop everywhere you go or must conduct some business while you are traveling, leave it at home. It will be heavy to carry, and your accommodations may not have great security.

Use an Internet café to communicate with friends, family, or physicians while abroad. Many Internet cafés charge a minimal fee and can be much less expensive than calling long distance.

Most digital cameras will not work at an Internet café. You may not be able to send pictures or videos, depending on your location.

Leisure Time

Chances are you will not be able to find a television that broadcasts in English. Leisure time may vary. You may have very little spare time, or you may spend a lot of time in your hotel room.

Bring at least one good book. It may be hard to find any in English. Other actives may include playing cards, hobbies such as cross-stitch or drawing, or business-related activities.

Other miscellaneous items you may want to bring include the following:

- Foreign language phrase book
- Infant or child carrier
- Insect repellent
- Nightlight
- Sewing kit

- Shopping bags
- Small flashlight
- Stroller/umbrella stroller
- Tape
- Travel alarm clock
- Travel guide
- Zippered plastic bags

Chapter 19

Clothing to Pack

You will want to pack weather-appropriate clothing that respects the customs and traditions of your host country. Taste and discretion in your clothing choices are good rules to follow. Think business casual to professional. Suits or dresses are not necessary, except possibly for your court appearance. Dressy-casual clothing should include khaki or dark chinos, skirts, and polo shirts.

You may find that you will want or need to visit two different cites, regions, or countries. These may include where your child is residing and where you must travel to visit the U.S. Embassy to receive your visa before returning home. Temperatures and weather may vary. The temperature in Moscow was 70 degrees, while just 500 miles south it was 100 degrees. Because it was summer, we took a nice pair of shorts, but they are sometimes recommended even during winter months. You may need to take shorts for loungewear; the heating in your hotel may be very warm.

Your host government may control the heating systems, and if you travel in September or October, you may find yourself in hotels or apartments without heat. The same holds true in the spring when the heat has been turned off, but there is still cool weather.

There are many myths about proper dress for adoption travel. For example, Europeans wear only black; do not take tennis shoes; or dress children dressed in long pants and long-sleeved tops and hats. Being extremely fashion-conscious, I was worried about all the things that I had heard about inappropriate clothing and found that (at least on this trip) little of it was actually true.

However, the type of clothing considered appropriate will vary from one city or region to the next. Some will be tourist destinations or resort cities that are accustomed to tourists. More traditional or rural locations require more conservative clothing. Cultural requirements may mean that women must wear scarves, head coverings, skirts, or dresses when touring local cathedrals or other religious sites.

What to Take

You will be judged by how you conduct yourself and how you are dressed. It is usually not considered appropriate to wear jeans on your first visit to the orphanage. This would also apply if you must first visit government offices before you are allowed to meet your child.

When selecting an outfit to wear to court, choose one that will make a good impression while showing proper respect for the court. Although it is not necessary to wear a suit, clothes options for men would include pants, a button-up shirt, tie and jacket. For women, a dress or skirt set would be most appropriate.

More versatility in dressing may be obtained by choosing a skirt set and other clothing that can coordinate with it. This will give you flexibility and clothing options while packing a minimal number of pieces. Take items that can be layered and are wrinkle resistant. Most likely, you will need to take two outfits per person and wear a third while traveling. We also took several articles of clothing that would coordinate with other items to dress up or down as needed. I chose a dressy sheer cardigan that would give my black skirt and blouse an evening look.

Comfortable basic walking shoes are essential. Tennis shoes or other sport shoes may or may not be considered appropriate. It may depend on their color. White shoes would be much more noticeable than black ones. You may want to take slippers to wear when you are in your hotel and possibly shower shoes or flip-flops for the shower.

Sweat suits, shorts, and T-shirts are only suitable for lounging in your hotel room. Jeans should be okay to wear while traveling or during other non-business aspects of your trip, but don't take more than one pair. Black denim will provide you with a more sophisticated look than blue.

Warm-Weather Travel

The term *warm-weather travel* may be relevant if you are traveling to northern Russia or Siberia. All-weather coats or jackets may be necessary as weather can change unexpectedly. At the same time, you may find sweltering temperatures whether you travel to Russia or Guatemala in the summer.

Even if temperatures are very warm, a sweater or jacket should be taken for use on the plane, indoor locations that are blessed with air conditioners, or where it is common to find a large discrepancy in day and evening temperatures.

Areas that are accustomed to warm weather should be more prepared for providing relief from the heat than countries such as Russia where it is rare to find air conditioning in many houses, hotels, and other locations. In addition to taking essentials, you may want to pack several extra tops and underwear. If it's very hot, you may need to change clothes more often.

Lightweight, breathable fabrics are best. Natural fabrics may be cooler than synthetic ones, but they will not travel as well and may wrinkle easily. Skirts may be cooler than pants and look nicer, too. Shoes should be comfortable; remember that excessive heat may cause your feet to swell. Use caution when considering sandals or other open-toed shoes.

You may have the opportunity to visit beaches and lakes or use hotel pools if you are traveling during summer months. My husband decided to take a swimsuit since we were traveling in midsummer, and one of our hotels had an indoor pool. At the last minute I threw mine in the suitcase since there was enough room. I was very happy to have made this decision, though I was very skeptical about it at first, the gamble paid off. While we did not use the pool at our hotel, we were taken to the local beach for a swim in the Volga River, which is considered good luck.

A basic warm-weather wardrobe for women should include the following:

- 1 print skirt
- 1 basic black skirt
- 1 pair of casual pants
- 1 blouse
- 1 two-piece cardigan set
- 1 knit shirt
- 1 light/crocheted sweater

Extra items could include a pair of shorts and a knit shirt, a swimsuit, and a dressy blouse or sweater.

For men, the wardrobe should include these items:

- 1 pair of shorts
- 1 pair of khaki pants
- 1 pair of dress slacks
- 1 knit shirt
- 1 polo shirt
- 1 casual shirt

Also include a dress shirt, tie and blazer for court, and possibly a swimsuit and a T-shirt.

Cold-Weather Travel

You should be able to find current weather forecasts from a variety of sources to help you make your selections when packing. Unless you are traveling to climates with mild winters, winter coats should be full-length. It can be very cool in the fall, and some areas may see first snows as early as late September. Winter temperatures in Eastern Europe can vary from those in the northern United States to an Arctic expedition.

Hats are a basic requirement from October through March, and no one will let you outside without a head covering. Plan on taking a good pair of gloves and a scarf. Boots should be lined and water-resistant, and you should plan on taking a second pair of shoes wherever you go to change into when you go inside.

Lightweight thermal underwear may be necessary, and tights and leggings can be worn under pants or skirts for extra warmth. You may need to insulate yourself for warmth outside, but it may be very warm inside. It may be necessary to remove a layer or two of clothing whenever you are indoors. You do not want to wear just a thermal shirt underneath a wool sweater, because you would probably not be able to remove your sweater as needed.

A basic cold-weather wardrobe for women should include:
- 1 long skirt
- 1 pair of casual pants
- 1 pair of denim pants
- 1 blouse
- 1 turtleneck sweater
- 1 turtleneck
- 1 wool blazer
- 1 cardigan sweater
- 1 sweater
- 1 dressy sweater or blouse

The wardrobe for men should include:

- 1 pair of casual pants
- 1 pair of nice slacks
- 1 pair of jeans
- 1 long-sleeved knit shirt
- 1 oxford shirt
- 1 turtleneck
- 1 sweater or cardigan
- 1 sweater vest
- 1 pullover sweater
- 1 wool blazer, dress shirt, and tie

The Worst Clothing Mistake

The worst clothing mistake I made on our trip to Russia was not taking sneakers. I have permanent foot damage from wearing high heels for too many years while working in the retail industry. When I am on my feet a long time, it is not a question of whether my feet will hurt but how bad the pain will be.

We were at our daughter's orphanage several hours in the morning and evening and were standing outside primarily on asphalt. We visited parks and other tourist areas during the day. Unfortunately, I was not able to do anything in the evenings because my feet hurt too badly to walk anywhere else. The two pairs of shoes I took were my most comfortable sandals and a pair of heels.

It was also 104 degrees the day we went to court, and I wore a long black skirt, sleeveless blouse, and a long-sleeved black cardigan. This was the outfit I took specifically for court. When our facilitator picked us up that day, she was wearing a backless top with crepe pants. She did not accompany us inside the courtroom, but we did not know that until we arrived.

Our entire female staff wore dresses above the knee—even a sleeveless red dress—90 percent of the time. I saw people wearing Capri pants and handkerchief skirts, shorts, and other fashion-forward clothes in an assortment of colors, and yes, tennis shoes.

Apparently because of the heat, no one wore slips, and many panty lines were showing—for the younger women, these were mostly thongs. Waitresses wore very, very short skirts, and I was "mooned" by one who tried to wake up a guy who had passed out at breakfast on our first morning in the region.

There must have been a law concerning the wearing of white blouses. Apparently if you wear a white blouse, you are required to wear the laciest bra available underneath it. This included all Aeroflot flight attendants. Of course we also saw the traditional Babushkas in housedresses and scarves during our travels.

Fortunately, at the last minute, I threw a pair of shorts and a swimsuit into our suitcase. Of course, in my tankini top and skirt bottom, I was completely overdressed when we visited the beach. The bottom line is wear what you are comfortable in. Take a nice outfit for court and don't spend too much time and energy worrying about clothing.

No one ever made us feel uncomfortable or made negative comments. Unless you are fluent in your child's native language, your ability to blend will be over the minute you open your mouth and everyone will know you are not a native. If you don't believe me, just ask all the people who asked us what time it was or for directions.

Clothing for Your Child

You will need to provide all of your child's clothing needs. This usually includes the clothes that he wears when he leaves the orphanage or from the time you receive custody of him. The clothing you will need for your child will be similar to what you need. These items include pajamas, underwear and undershirts, thermals, coats or snowsuits, scarves, hats, gloves or mittens, street clothes, sweaters or jackets, shoes, and socks. (See Chapter 4, "The Toddler Wardrobe.")

When you are granted custody of your child, it is a special occasion and most likely you will want to pack a special "going home/leaving the hospital" outfit. Your child's caretakers will be watching closely to make sure that your child is appropriately dressed. Less is not more, and you will need to provide the appropriate number of layers deemed necessary for your child to be adequately protected from the elements.

Toddlers and infants are not allowed outdoors in many societies without a hat, and failing to bring one or have your child wear one may mean that you proceed at your own risk. More than a few ignorant Americans have been scolded for these offenses.

Because it was summer when we adopted Callie, I took dresses, sweaters, and hats. With these in tow, I had my bases covered. We did not know if shorts would be considered inappropriate or if we would be reprimanded if she did not have on long sleeves or a hat.

Of course, the hats were too big, as were most of the clothes. Callie was much smaller than we thought. Dresses and jumpers for girls and elastic-waist pants for boys will help minimize the problem. I recommend taking approximately five or six outfits. Take one that is a size smaller than your estimate, three the size you estimate your child is, and one or two a size larger. If you have time, you could buy some things there, but I would plan on taking at least 75 percent of your child's clothing needs because you may not have time to shop.

Take clothing that can be removed easily and quickly. Callie was sick on the plane to Moscow and had worn three dresses that morning by the time we got to the American Embassy.

Laundry

Because you will be limited in the amount of clothing that you will be able to pack, you will want to take wrinkle-resistant clothing in quick-drying wash-and-wear fabrics. Plan on doing at least part or all of your laundry yourself, so you will need a small box of laundry detergent, a clothesline, and a sink stopper.

Powdered detergent is best. Most likely, you will not be able to use tablets since most of your wash will be done in your sink. For delicates, take liquid delicate care cleaner or use shampoo. For example, shampoo for color-treated hair is designed specifically to stay colorfast. Most laundries sell small travel-size or single-use packages of detergent. Pack detergent in a zippered bag to prevent spills.

Thank goodness for laundry service. We were able to get same-day laundry service at two of our three hotels. (We did not ask at the third.) We would give the hotel staff our clothes in the morning and they were returned to us clean in the evening. Because we had taken three complete outfits, we could wear one, have one in the laundry being cleaned, and one for a backup in case we needed to change. The downside to laundry service is that it may be expensive. We found laundry to be like most things—the bigger the city, the bigger the bill.

Chapter 20

While You Are There

It is not unusual for families to find that adoption travel is the first time they travel outside the country. You may notice differences from the time you board your plane. Airline instructions may be given in English as well as another language. It would not be unusual to find that many people on your plane are native to your host country and that you may be an English-speaking minority.

When you land, you may be disoriented as a result of jet lag, anticipation, unfamiliar surroundings, or insecurity at not knowing the language. It can be intimidating to enter a foreign country, especially if you are greeted by armed guards at the gates before going through passport control and customs.

In most cases an agency representative will meet you as soon as you go through customs. Keep your emergency contact numbers handy in case just in case you are not able to find your contact. Most agencies wish to provide clients with the best possible service, and your safety is of the utmost concern.

Most likely, you will have a driver, interpreter, and facilitator who will be with you everywhere you go. Sometimes a driver will act as the interpreter as well. If this is the case, you may be charged two fees for his or her services. Another possibility is that two families who are completing an adoption simultaneously will both get charged the full fee for services, even though they are being performed at the same time.

It may or may not be possible to shop or sightsee without their services, and they will tell you what they recommend. It is possible that an agency may advise against or refuse to allow clients to do so on their own.

Whether you are traveling by land or by sea, try to absorb everything around you; this is a trip of a lifetime. You will see many things for the first and possibly only time. The sights, sounds, and even smells may take some getting used to. No amount of preparation can ever truly prepare you for this trip.

Having grown up relatively close to the Appalachian Mountains, I have been to homes without indoor plumbing. However, I never anticipated the overwhelming poverty of the orphanage or of the Russian Federation. The city where Callie was born is a wonderful city, which we thoroughly enjoyed. It is also the capital of the region and would not be considered particularly poor or destitute. However, many homes do not have running water, and many roads and homes were in desperate need of repair. Unfortunately, there is little money.

Even so, we found that the pride and passion of the Russian people was alive and well. While they may struggle to afford material things, they are rich in culture and tradition. Your adoption travel should include as much exposure to your child's culture as possible. As your child grows, you will find that her heritage is very important to her, and you have a responsibility to reinforce this pride.

Adoption as Viewed by the People

The majority of people we met in Russia were very glad that the children were finding a home, and we found ourselves being in the unique position of being admired for what we were undertaking, even though it was for purely selfish reasons.

Attitudes about adoption may sometimes appear controversial, but no country wants to admit to having a social crisis where poverty and lack of health care helps increase the number of children who may be abandoned, abused, or neglected. It is not uncommon for even seasoned adoption professionals to be overcome by the sheer magnitude of the problem.

You will find that some countries are less adoption-friendly than others. Residents of your host country may not understand why you would want to adopt a child or sibling group who may be older, who may be considered a social outcast, or who, they believe, has a genetic predisposition to be "difficult" or has special needs.

Many people believe that foreigners should not adopt children, no matter what their circumstances. It is not uncommon for unfounded rumors about adoption to take place; one popular one is that the children's organs are being sold. This belief may be exacerbated by a lack of understanding.

You may find that local residents do not believe that there is anything wrong with housing children indefinitely in an orphanage. It is not uncommon for orphanages to house children who are not legal orphans but instead have been sent by parents who can not afford to feed or clothe them. Family members regularly visit many children in orphanages in Eastern Europe, which prevents them from being adopted. Infrequently, if birth families find out about an impending adoption, they may come forward to "reclaim" a child, at least temporarily, to prevent his adoption.

As adoptive parents, it is our responsibility to be gracious and to conduct ourselves in an exemplary manner particularly while completing an adoption. You are, in a sense, an ambassador of good will for your country, and you set the standard on how adoptive parents are viewed.

Homestays

We never really considered a "homestay" or staying with a host family. However, many people enjoy the cultural experience of getting a feel for the everyday life of the people of the country.

Apartments in Russia are not very large or private. They frequently have one bedroom, a kitchen, living room, and bathroom. Your host may stay with friends or family while you stay in his or her home. However, it is not unusual for your host to sleep on the couch while you sleep in the bedroom.

Consider why you are there and ask yourself if you would you prefer to be in a hotel. You may have to make difficult decisions regarding your adoption, have jet lag, suffer from fatigue, feel unwell, or be unhappy with your staff or agency. In addition, do you want someone else present when you are bonding with your child? The upside for an older child would be having an interpreter around while you are getting to know each other. The downside is that the host could interfere with this process.

Food is usually included in host stays, and your host may cook for you. This also may limit your options. On one trip, my friend Claire ate borscht for a week, and on another she had a large variety of very good food.

Homestays are usually much cheaper than a hotel and may be your only option depending on the size of the city, hotel availability, and your adoption agency.

Hotels

Hotel reservations are frequently made by your adoption agency, and they frequently negotiate adoption rates for families. Naturally, you may find that hotels in prime locations are more expensive. If cost is not a factor, you may wish to take the opportunity to splurge and stay in a very nice hotel.

Hotel reservations, which require a credit card number, may need to be made directly by the adoptive family. It is not uncommon to arrive and find other adoptive families staying at the same hotel.

Hotels frequently include breakfast and may or may not have one or more restaurants. The hotel staff may or may not speak English. Exchange rates are usually lower and souvenirs are usually more expensive, but sometimes the convenience is worth it. Hotels may offer a variety of services including restaurants, bars, nightclubs, casinos, swimming pools, exercise rooms, laundry services, and more.

Hotels considered moderate, budget, or economy may not be what we are used to by American standards. Don't think Hampton Inn; visualize indoor camping. Double beds in hotels in Eastern Europe are frequently two twin beds pushed together. If you request a suite, it will usually consist of one bedroom, a small living area, and a bathroom. You may or may not have a kitchen but will probably have a refrigerator and a television.

You need to request a crib when you make the reservation; they may or may not be available. Your child may have to sleep with you or you may have to be creative in finding another alternative. I know of one family who made "cribs" out of cardboard boxes lined with blankets for their very young toddlers.

If it is summer, you may have to request an air-conditioned room, if they are available. Windows may or may not have screens. You should do a basic safety inspection of your room to make sure that it will be safe for your child. Check electrical outlets, loose electrical cords, or cords on window blinds. Check windows and doors. Open windows, windows without screens, floor-level windows, and balcony doors all pose a danger to inquisitive toddlers.

Families who adopt from Guatemala may find that their hotel accommodations are similar to an oceanside resort with lush tropical foliage and gardens. Chinese and Cambodian adoptive families may expect to find hotels similar to many Western accommodations. Most large cities such as Beijing, Moscow, and St. Petersburg have their share of five-star hotels. While many adoptive families cannot afford to pay $200 a night for a hotel room, especially for an extended period, it can be well worth it to pay the extra for a night or two—especially if you have been in a remote region for any length of time.

We spent one week with 100-plus temperatures, no air conditioning, no screens on the windows, no ice (except what we started making from bottled water), and ate meat and potatoes three meals a day. The breakfast buffet at the Grand Marriott was almost overwhelming after having little or no selection. It was also the only hotel that I considered to be Western, and it was well worth the price.

When we were in Russia, our hotels had security guards at the elevators, and we had to show our hotel pass to be admitted onto the elevators. The biggest problem with safety and security is property theft. Do not leave valuables in your hotel room and keep your suitcases locked whenever you are out.

Many hotels have floor ladies or maids. In Russia, they were on duty at all times and basically knew who was coming and going. They saw to needs such as more towels, toilet paper, laundry services, etc. Floor ladies should be tipped generously. I wanted to take one home as a souvenir.

Visiting the Orphanage and Meeting Your Child

The first thing that you will want to do after you arrive is meet your child. Whether you are able to do this immediately will depend on the time of your arrival, if you must first visit local government agencies prior to your visitation, and the adoption procedure in your host country.

Remember to dress accordingly; do not wear jeans during your first visit. You may meet the orphanage director and other members of the staff during this visit, and it is important to make a good first impression. This visit will be overwhelming and has been known to bring even the strongest of men to tears. If possible, try to get a member of the staff or another family who may be traveling with you to record or take pictures of this first meeting.

During the first meetings (and possibly subsequent ones), your child may be scared or intimidated. She may be attached to a caregiver who is less than thrilled about the prospect of handing her over to you. It is also possible that she may never have spent any time around a male or that something may remind her of a previous negative experience. It is also possible that she is as overwhelmed as you may be.

During this first meeting, you will probably want to bring a few toys or treats to use as ice breakers. I took a small doll and a ball. Callie was shy at first, but after I pulled out the doll, we were in. The three of us played ball and laughed and played on the slide until it was time to go. We let Callie take the doll with her, and as we watched her join her group that day, she took it and showed it to her caretaker. We never saw the doll again and this is not uncommon. Usually anything you send in with your child will not come back out. Buy duplicates or triplicates of anything you consider special. You may want to buy one to give on the first meeting, and the second for everyday use to take with you on future visits or after your adoption is completed. A third one could be for your memory box.

How often you are allowed to visit and how much time you are allowed to spend with your child will vary. We were able to visit twice a day for two hours at a time. Another family we met was traveling with a second family whose child was in another orphanage, so they had to split time between the two orphanages. That family only got to visit about thirty minutes a day.

During our visits, we played outdoors and I took two or three toys per visit with us. Where your visits are conducted and the availability of other toys and possible interaction with other children may determine your needs. You may want to take snacks or other treats and favorite toys, and you may need enough to share. We took bubbles, crayons and a coloring book, books, a doll, and a beanbag cat.

One book was about moving your body parts. I had learned the parts of the body in Russian, so we could read and played together. Callie's favorite toy was a small turtle that played "Twinkle, Twinkle Little Star," and she played it repeatedly. (Don't forget extra batteries!) Because it was so hot, we drank bottled water all the time, and she thoroughly enjoyed learning how to drink from a water bottle and playing with it.

We found the orphanage to be poor but neat, clean, and in much need of repair. Children age one to three resided there, and there were five boys in Callie's group. She was the only girl, and it was obvious that she was well taken care of. Her caretakers were proud to be her momma, and I saw them hug her, pick her up, and even kiss her. I also saw one who was very fond of Callie give her a piece of candy. In total, we met three different caretakers, but only one is probably on duty at a time.

We met the director of the orphanage briefly to give her our orphanage donations and take a small tour. We also met with the doctor on two different occasions. She was at the orphanage at least four days that we saw, but I suspect that there is a doctor on duty at all times.

Declining a Referral

It is possible that you may be faced with a difficult decision regarding the continuation of your adoption. Families can and, infrequently, do decide to decline a referral after they meet the child in person. Sometimes the chemistry is not there, but most often families will discover that the child has a medical condition that they are not equipped to handle.

Make arrangements to contact your adoption medical specialist or pediatrician if necessary so you can make an informed decision. It may be possible to contact a local doctor who can evaluate the child in person.

Declining a referral is never easy and will require a great deal of soul searching. As painful as this may be, you must make a decision that is best for you, your family, and the child in question. In most cases, families who have declined a child have been able to continue with the adoption process and have been matched with a different child. Most of them will tell you that this was the child that was meant to be theirs.

Questions for the Caretaker

This may be the only time you are able to get information from anyone who has personal knowledge of and has interacted with your child or who has access to your child's records. Make the most of it and ask as many questions as possible. Take notes or record it if possible. Make sure that your questions are answered to your satisfaction. This may be quite challenging when using an interpreter who may be speaking English as a second language, but it may be your only opportunity. Here are some questions to consider.

Medical and Family History
- What vaccinations has your child received?
- What medical testing has he had?
- What are his known medical problems, and the current diagnosis, prognosis or recommended treatment?
- What childhood illness or other illnesses has he had? Has he been hospitalized or had surgery?
- What is his average temperature?
- Are there any scars (what caused these?) or birthmarks?
- Are there any known allergies?
- How does the child act when sick?
- What was the medical diagnosis at birth?
- Was the child born premature or at full term?
- Is there any history of prenatal alcohol or drug exposure or abuse?
- Why was the child placed for adoption?
- How long has he been at the orphanage?
- Is any personal information available about the birth family/siblings?
- Are there any special skills or therapy that we should observe/learn before we are granted custody?

Daily Activities
- What is your child's daily routine?
- What time does she get up?
- When is bedtime and how long does she sleep?
- Does she nap? How often and how long?
- What type of bed does she sleep in?
- May we see her room/living quarters?
- Does she sleep in a room or bed with other children?
- Are the lights on or off and is it quiet or noisy?
- How much and how often does she eat?
- What foods does she like or dislike?
- What foods are served at typical meals?
- What about snacks or treats?
- Does she drink from a bottle or cup?
- Does she drink cow's milk or formula?
- Is she fed or does she feed herself?
- How does she react when she is tired or hungry?
- Is the child potty trained and what is her bathroom routine? How are baths given? (Tub or showers, hot or cold water?)
- When is playtime and what are her favorite playtime activities or toys?
- Does she spend time outside?
- Does she have any personal possessions or things that are her that we can keep and replace for you?
- Does she know numbers, letters, or colors?
- Has she ever been around animals: cats and dogs?
- Has the child ever ridden in a car, used a car seat?

Child Development
- Can your child talk or use other nonverbal communication?
- At what age did he reach developmental milestones: talking, walking, etc.?
- Is he afraid of anything, or do you have other emotional concerns?

•How is he comforted when upset?
•Is he attached to a caregiver? Does he have or has he had a favorite playmate?
•What are the names of caretakers/friends?
•Does he get along with other children, adults?
•Is he affectionate or dislike physical contact?
•Does he have good eye contact?
•How does he react when being scolded?
•What type of discipline is used? How does he respond?
•What is the child's normal personality? Shy, aggressive, outgoing?
•How does he compare to other children his age in the home?

Miscellaneous
•Has the child been baptized or participated in other religious ceremonies?
•Are there any keepsakes or records of this?
•Who named the child?
•What is her ethnic background?
•Are there any photographs available?
•Are complete copies of his file available?
•Would anyone care to write a letter for your child?
•Is it possible to remain in contact with the orphanage or other associates? What is the address?
•What types of updates would they like to receive?
•Why has he not been adopted before now?

Orphanage Donations

The orphanage's need for basic essentials was far greater than we could have imagined. It was hard to plan for orphanage donations in advance because it is difficult to fully comprehend these needs without actually seeing them for yourself, and I ended up feeling as though many of the things that I had taken were not as useful as others might have been.

We brought some gifts us for the orphanage but bought many of the things that they needed once we arrived. Some people choose to take money and buy what they need. If you have to travel twice, you should be able to find out specific individual needs. Clothing overseas may be cheaper, and you may be able to buy more, but you can purchase better quality merchandise in the United States.

Shop at discount stores or stores that specialize in overruns. Look for end-of-season sales of overstocked merchandise. I recently purchased infant and toddler boys' two-piece sweat suits for $3 from a local discount store and purchased approximately thirty summer outfits for around $75 last fall. If you have children's clothing or merchandise manufacturers in your area, call them. Sometimes stores or business will donate new merchandise, seconds, or overruns to you or an organization that you may be affiliated with that is collecting orphanage donations.

You may get better results if you enlist the help of your office staff, women's club, school, or church to help collect donations. Don't think you can't ask for contributions. Instead you must decide that it never hurts to ask. I was able to get an extra 50 percent off summer clearance merchandise, toothbrushes from the dentist, and latex gloves from my doctor's office. My women's club at church collected orphanage donations as our international project, and my husband and I took them to Russia on second adoption trip.

If you are using fundraising or other means to help fund an adoption, this may be a great way to help cover some of these expenses. If this is the case, this information should be included when the organization is considering your proposal.

When we visited the orphanage, we were given a list of needed items, and food was not on the list. We were asked to buy prescription medication and very basic clothing including infant pants (better than onesies, they said), T-shirts, underwear, and blankets. I insisted on buying a dozen pairs of toddler underwear, and many times we witnessed the children wearing just their underwear and sometimes a T-shirt. They could have used a lot of T-shirts and shorts.

The clothing or shoes the children wore could not have been sold at a resale shop. They had been washed and worn many times, and the colors were faded. Callie often had shoes on that were too small. We took five pairs of shoes in different sizes and left the three that were too small for Callie. She wore a toddler size seven.

The best shoes to take are the generic kind for boys or girls. The kind with Velcro closures rather than buckles or laces is preferable. Leather lasts longer and will stay dryer than canvas in wet or snowy weather. The best sizes to take are sizes four to eight.

Our staff was very conscious about how much money we spent. They did not want us to overspend. I would have bought much more for the orphanage if time had allowed and if I had had a better understanding of how much I was spending at the time. I can say that at the orphanage, the need for shoes and other essentials far outweighed the need for toys. The orphanage appeared to have plenty of toys. However, if you want to take toys, don't take more than one or two nice ones, unless you know that they have a specific need or they have made a request. Toys should help enhance child development. Blocks or toys that play music, have buttons, or make noises are best. Remember replacing batteries will probably be impossible because they cannot afford to buy them, so take extras.

You may find that certain well-known brands such as Legos or Barbie may be popular. I do not recommend taking plush animals. They are hard to clean, and I have seldom seen them in an orphanage. Toys should include animals and real people versus cartoon characters, monsters, or other creatures.

In most cases orphanage donations should be new items. Do not take previously used clothing or other items without permission from your adoption agency. If this is acceptable, they should be gently used and in good to excellent condition. Limit large bulky items such as diapers, which may be hard to pack, or other items that may be too heavy. You should be able to purchase diapers when you arrive.

Check to make sure any medication you plan to take for a donation is legal in your host country. If they are not legal, they may be confiscated by customs. Your agency should be able to tell you if a product can be used, if they have translated instructions for use, and whether the doctors would be familiar with its usage.

If you are taking a large amount of donations, it may be necessary to obtain a letter from your adoption agency stating that you are carrying orphanage donations. Having this letter with separately boxed items clearly marked *orphanage donations* or *humanitarian aid* may help you avoid paying customs fees. If you exceed luggage limitations, you may be charged for an extra container, by weight.

You may also find that you are expected to purchase some items even though you had not been notified in advance and had brought donations with you. Because of this, you should not plan on purchasing more than half of donations in advance without specific instructions from your agency.

Some adoption fees may include orphanage donations and it may not be necessary to make additional donations. However if you choose to, they are always appreciated. Ideas for donations include:

Clothing
- •Coats or snowsuits
- •Dresses
- •Gloves, mittens
- •Hats, scarves
- •Pants, shirts
- •Shoes and socks
- •Sweaters or jackets
- •Tights
- •Toddler underwear
- •T-shirts
- •Two-piece clothing

Essentials
- Baby food, formula, or cereal
- Baby soap, shampoo, and lotion
- Bibs
- Blankets
- Bottles and nipples, including those for children with cleft lip and palate
- Diapers
- Hair brushes/combs
- Hand towels, hooded towels
- Latex gloves
- Snack food for older toddlers
- Toothbrushes and toothpaste
- Vitamins or medication

Toys
- Beach balls (they pack flat and can be blown up) or other balls
- Blocks
- Books
- Crib mobile
- Developmental toys
- Paper, pencils and crayons
- Puzzles
- Sand pails
- Tape recorder and cassette tapes

Gifts

Gift giving as a way of expressing thanks or gratitude is quite common in many cultures. Although customary, gifts do not have to be expensive but should be thoughtful and in good taste. Your agency will tell you for whom you may need to purchase gifts. Most likely, you will need gifts for your homestay host, facilitators, drivers, translators, and orphanage workers. In addition to these, the nicest gifts should be given to the judge, orphanage director, assistant director, or possible other representatives. You may also consider small gifts for floor ladies, maids, hotel staff, or tour guides.

Your facilitator will instruct you on how gift giving should be conducted. He may wish to look at the gift items and give you his recommendation, or all gifts may be given to him and he will give them on your behalf at his discretion. This may or may not be in your presence. It is possible that when you arrive you will find out that giving gifts to certain individuals is no longer considered appropriate; in that case it may be easier to give them away rather than take them home with you.

Gifts should include items that you would like to receive and should be useful. Gifts or items that we take for granted may be considered a luxury item. If you are traveling on two separate trips, you may take a few small gifts for the first trip. However, you should wait until after the adoption to give gifts to people who can directly affect the adoption process. If you are traveling on two trips, you will be able to select more personalized individual gifts. You may find that you receive gifts as well.

Gifts should not be wrapped because they may be unwrapped at customs or baggage check. Gift bags and tissue pack easily, and the bags can be reused. Small, clear cellophane party bags with designs on them can be purchased at most paper or party supply stores. Party bags can be filled ahead of time because they are see-through, and you should not have to open them. If you do need to open them, it is as simple as untying the ribbon. I used cloth ribbon to tie these with so that the recipient could reuse it.

Items that are homemade or native to where you live make great gifts, and it would be less likely that they may have been received before. Local canned foods such as apple butter or maple syrup, wine from a local vineyard, cassette tapes containing regional music or that of a local group or individual that you know, Native American jewelry or other items that may reflect your heritage, and books or souvenirs from your city or state all make unique gifts. It may also be possible to purchase items such as flowers or chocolate that may be considered a luxury item.

Most gifts should cost between $5 to $25 and could include the following:
•American whiskey/bourbon
•Bottled dry spices
•Candy
•Candy dish
•Car accessories
•Cassette tapes
•Cigarettes
•Clocks
•Coffee and specialty teas
•Cookies
•Cosmetics/Perfume or cologne
•Dish towels
•Folding umbrellas
•Gloves
•Hot chocolate
•Kitchen gadgets
•Manicure sets
•Office supplies
•Pens or pencil sets
•Quality costume jewelry
•Scarves
•Slippers
•Stationery/note cards
•Tote bags
•Travel mugs
•Watches

Gifts for children may include:
•Action figures
•Barbie
•Bubbles
•Balloons
•Coloring books/crayons
•Chocolate/candy
•Construction paper
•hair bows
•Hot Wheels cars
•Jump ropes
•Lollipops
•Popular movie items

Souvenirs

Each region or area of a country may have certain souvenir items that are unique. You may find that regional souvenirs may be a better quality and that the prices may be more reasonable than those found in larger cities and tourist areas.

I only bought a few things while in the region, but I wish I had gotten more because the quality was very good. They included a small matryoshka that has scenes from the city, a Roly Poly (a doll that can not fall over with a chime inside), and a traditional hand-painted sake glass, which was a wooden decorative piece that was beautifully painted and shaped like a person. I never saw anything like it anywhere else. Unfortunately it was a gift for a friend, and I did not buy one for myself.

Other gifts that I bought included a shawl, an assortment of matryoshka dolls, lacquer boxes, serving trays, matryoshka key chains, pens, and pencils, Christmas ornaments, two hand-sewn traditional Russian dresses for Callie, handmade dolls, Gzhel porcelain, playing cards, a journal, a T-shirt, a book of folk tales, and of course vodka.

I am a big shopper, and I bought so much that our luggage weighed more going home than when we went. I had packed gifts and other belongings in several small boxes, which I then used to pack souvenirs for the return trip. Several of these were plastic shoeboxes. Nothing broke, but I'd suggest purchasing newspaper to wrap items in or taking a small amount of bubble wrap.

Going to Court

Whether you are required to attend an adoption hearing will depend on the country. In some countries, either one or both parents must attend the court proceeding while others may be conducted without your physical presence. Adoption hearings range in seriousness from a technicality to a complex review of the case.

Appearing in court to complete your adoption can be the most intimidating part of the process. The judge, a court reporter, a court-approved interpreter, the chief doctor from the orphanage, who testified on Callie's medical condition, a prosecutor who is an advocate for the child, and a representative from the overseeing government agency who may testify to the authenticity of the documentation were all present during our adoption hearing. No one from the adoption agency or any member of our staff appeared in the courtroom with us.

Our judge was very formal and did not smile until after the ruling. Apparently Russians view biological children and adopted children differently and many questions focused on how we felt about this or that since she was not our biological child. You may also be asked questions concerning infertility, possible birth of biological children, why you want to adopt, how you plan to help preserve their heritage, child-care, finances, or home ownership. If you are a single parent, you will be asked similar questions. In addition, you may hear concerns about your ability to do this as a single parent, why you want to do this without a spouse, and infrequently, sexual orientation.

You may be instructed to testify that you had not been given a video or received other pertinent information about your referral before travel. While this may make you uneasy, it is not uncommon and, in most cases, is not considered unethical. It is often an unfortunate circumstance of how the system works; everyone knows it and everyone plays along.

The hearing only took about an hour, which included a twenty-minute recess to allow for the judge's decision. Mostly our court appearance was a formality. On occasion, you will find a prosecutor or a judge who is a stickler for paperwork, protocol, or procedures, and an adoption hearing may take a day or two.

Our judge wanted to have a legitimate, black-and-white reason to waive our ten-day waiting period. If this is an option and you are requesting this, you will need to have letters or statements from your physician, employer, or other applicable person. Of course, these will need to notarized and apostilled.

It is important that you dress appropriately. Women should wear a nice skirt or dress, and men should wear a coat and tie, but a formal suit is not necessary. Denim, no matter how dressy, is not appropriate court attire.

If you are nervous before your hearing, just imagine waking up very sick on the day of your adoption hearing. We did, and I can testify to the fact that there is nothing like an intestinal virus to take your mind off an impending court appearance.

Saying Good-bye

When it's time to take custody of your child, it can be quite emotional. It can signify the completion of years of trying to build a family. It can also be emotional for orphanage staff, foster parents, or other caregivers who may have formed a strong attachment to your child. They may be equally torn between being happy for your child and being saddened by their loss. Oftentimes the mood may be one of celebration, and it is not uncommon for as many workers as possible to see your child off. You will need to bring clothing for your child that is considered culturally appropriate. Most likely you would want this to be a special outfit, which will be a treasured keepsake.

You may receive a parting gift or memento of your child. If not, ask if there is an item of clothing or a favored possession that you can have. You may need to make a trade or purchase a replacement. For Callie, we have two beaded necklaces that were made by one of the orphanage workers.

When it was time to pick Callie up, our staff wanted me to do that while Mike completed some paperwork. Something was lost in the translation, and they thought Mike wanted us to go together and actually dress Callie in her new clothes when it was time for her to leave. What he actually meant was that he wanted to be there when we picked her up. Needless to say, we dressed her in the parking lot. When it was time to leave, we looked up to see people we watching from the windows.

Traveling with Your Child

When preparing to travel home with your child, it may feel like the climax of your trip, but in fact the real adventure is just beginning. Most likely, your child has never ridden in a car, train, or plane. Since you have no idea if your child is susceptible to motion sickness (or sensitive to new foods, as in our case), you may want to have an airsick bag on hand for emergencies.

He may never have been in a car seat or any type of seating where he was restrained for a short period—much less for an extended time. Children two and older must have their own airplane seat. If you are planning on using a car seat, you may want to try to help him become accustomed to sitting in it beforehand.

Changes in air pressure for young children who have had frequent ear infections can be painful. It is not uncommon to have crying babies on return flights, and they may be equally uncomfortable with their new surroundings and new parents.

If you are lucky, your toddler will sleep a large portion of your trip. Traveling as directly as possible will help relieve some of the fatigue. If you are traveling during your child's active time of day, you may find that you have to take walks up and down the aisles or try to hold him in your lap. For small toddlers, you may want to consider using a lap belt attachment during the flight.

In your carryon luggage, you should consider packing a baby blanket, sweater, one or two changes of clothes for your child, and one for each parent. To help pass the time, you should be armed with a variety of toys or treats for your toddler. A small child's backpack is a great way to carry these, and it could be carried within your diaper bag or other carry on luggage.

Chapter 21

Home Sweet Home

Some people have huge arrival parties at the airport, while others are simply greeted by immediate family. Adoptive families have varying travel experiences. Some will have short trips while others may be out of the country for an extended period. Families may have great trips that might include sightseeing, a quick court procedure, or a short stay; others have endured less desirable conditions, dealt with a difficult judge, or had various other problems. On the return trip home, some families may have minimized travel time by flying more direct routes while others may have traveled nonstop for twenty-four hours—possibly with a screaming or sick baby in tow.

Travel, fatigue, food- or waterborne illnesses, and the completion of the adoption process can all be overwhelming for new parents. Most likely, you will want to go home, eat, and sleep.

Before we had even stopped coasting down the runway, my husband spotted Grandma armed with a giant Winnie the Pooh and the rest of the grandparents plastered against the windows of the terminal.

Our plane arrived around lunchtime, and our parents drove us home where they had stocked our refrigerator and prepared lunch. We ate lunch and they were thrilled to visit with Callie, their first grandchild.

We were equally thrilled when they left a short time later so we could nap. Because your new arrival may have trouble adjusting to the time change or changes in his environment, it may be necessary to make prior arrangements with friends or family who can help while you are catching up on much needed rest and recuperation.

Meeting the New Arrival

Once friends and family learn that you are home, your phone will probably be ringing off the hook with well-wishers who want to come and visit. It is best to forewarn them of your plans.

You may want to have a nesting period and minimize outside contact. You need to establish yourself as the primary caretaker and may find it necessary to educate others regarding feeding or other physical contact with your child.

Start slowly by inviting a small intimate group of friends over. Avoid curiosity seekers or gossipmongers. Large groups or noise may overwhelm your child. By inviting too many people over at once, the focus shifts from meeting the new toddler to socializing between guests. The last thing you want to worry about is cooking, cleaning, or entertaining.

Many people who visit your new arrival will want to bring a present, even if they attended a baby shower. Try to limit the amount of gifts your child is given. If you are swamped with gifts, you may be able to tuck some away for future use.

Parenting

After you get home, you will discover that your work has only just begun. Each family member will need time to become acquainted with one another. You will have to establish new routines, and it will take time to figure out what your toddler's needs are. During this time, both you and your toddler may experience frustration, anger, or anxiety.

Many children experience grief or fear after leaving their old home, regardless of what the conditions may have been. Your toddler may be somewhat depressed or angry that you have taken her away from familiar surroundings, her caretakers, or other children. She may throw temper tantrums, cry, or otherwise act out her frustration. This frustration may be aimed at her primary caretaker, and it is not uncommon for children to show a preference for one parent over another.

Relationships with friends will change, and you may suddenly find yourself "on the outside looking in." This may be especially true if you have many childless friends. You will lose much of your ability to be spontaneous, and you may not be able to participate in social activities if you receive little advance notice. Simple things such as running to the grocery store may require scheduling and preparation, which could include finding a sitter, scheduling around naps, or packing a diaper bag.

If one parent is staying at home while the other returns to work, his or her lifestyle may change more significantly. The working parent may have a harder time adjusting to lifestyle changes in his or her nonworking hours because he has resumed his normal work schedule.

A working parent may not witness much of the child's normal routine or behavior and might be unaware of how any changes may affect the child. For example, this parent may not know that at 10:30, Susie gets a snack and that when she is hungry, she gets tired and irritable. The parent may assume that since it is only an hour and a half to lunchtime that she doesn't need a snack and can wait until then and eat.

In another scenario, the parent may think that snacks are treats and may decide that because Susie is grumpy or misbehaving that she can't have a treat. In both cases, hunger and the need to eat cause Susie's behavior. Instead of fixing the problem, it is aggravated.

Children need structure, and a working parent who is home all day on the weekends can throw a monkey wrench into the mix. One parent may not appreciate having to defer to the other parent's child-care expertise. Moreover, the child may ignore primary caretaker when the other parent is present. Single parents need a strong support system, which may include friends and family who have the same value system and can help fill in as needed.

Parents or caregivers often have different ideas about the importance of schedules as well as discipline and other parenting skills. These differences should be discussed before the adoption takes place because they can cause disagreements. Adoptive families must work together to fulfill their parenting responsibilities. At the same time, parents must also be allowed time to become parents. It may not be easy, but you will be able to find balance.

Post-Adoption Depression

Postpartum depression has long been attributed to changes in hormone levels after birth. However, a significant portion of adoptive parents report experiencing post-adoption depression (PAD). This often unrecognized form of depression might be unknown to health-care workers and adoption professionals.

The symptoms are the same as those for most forms of depression. They may include fatigue, irritability, loss of appetite, sadness, and a general sense of being overwhelmed. Individuals with a history of depression or families who have experienced failed adoptions or the loss of a referral may be at higher risk for PAD and may be more likely to experience it.

Finalizing an adoption is an emotional climax to perhaps years of trying to build a family. The stress of the process may be replaced by the new stress of caring for your child. PAD may be affected by unresolved infertility issues, physical demands of your child, changes in peer relationships, fear of legal issues arising with the adoption, or health problems (yours or your child's).

These feelings are not uncommon and will pass. However, because PAD can negatively affect attachment and bonding, it is important to seek help as necessary, which may include professional aid or friends and family who can help. Your needs and available resources will the level of help you seek.

Health Care

If you have not preregistered your child for health-care coverage, you need to do so immediately. If you have group health-care coverage, you have only thirty days from the date the adoption was completed to enroll your child for health insurance. You should follow up and make sure that your human resources representatives have completed the enrollment and remind them of the limitation.

Denial of coverage or classifying an adopted child as having a pre-existing condition is not allowed by group health coverage under the Health Insurance and Portability and Accountability Act of 1996. Families who are independent business owners or those who work for a small company and are not covered by a group insurance plan are not covered by this act and need to know their options. You should research your insurance policy and provisions because there are some exceptions. Always document your conversation and note the name of the person you spoke with.

Fielding Adoption Questions

Anyone who knows you are in the adoption process or meets your new child will have plenty of personal questions or comments. These questions will be asked regardless of your child's presence, age, and comprehension level, and without consideration of his or her feelings.

Disclose only the information you wish to and answer only those questions you are comfortable with. If you feel that questions are inappropriate, do not answer. Inappropriate questions may include what happened to his real parents, what do you know about his real parents, how much did it (the adoption) or he (your child) cost, why was he in an orphanage?

You will soon learn to tell the difference between people who are generally interested in adoption and those who are curiosity seekers or looking for a juicy story. One option to fielding adoption questions is to respond, "If you are interested in adoption, call me and I would be happy to talk to you about it or send you some information." If you are being pushed for answers, asking, "Why do you want to know?" may help, and for those who are truly obnoxious, there is always the "that's none of your business" or "this is a private family matter" answer.

You have probably already been told countless negative adoption stories about medical problems, disrupted adoptions, or stories about people who get pregnant after they adopt. Unfortunately, these stories do not stop once you have completed your adoption.

Generally attitudes regarding adoptive children include the belief that there must be something wrong with the child, that she was abandoned, abused, or neglected, or that you are a great and courageous person who went halfway around the world to give this child a home and she must be eternally grateful because you "saved her."

Often well-meaning people will not understand an adoptive family's sensitivity to negative adoption language, and it is our added responsibly to help teach positive adoption language. I recently spoke to an adult adoptee who referred to his birth mom as his "real" mom. On another occasion, I was annoyed enough to ask the pediatrician's office if my child was considered unnatural since the question was stated, "Is this your natural child?" as opposed to using the term *birth child*.

Preparing for questions in advance will help alleviate some of the awkwardness that you may feel when faced with confrontation. Just when you think you may have heard it all, you will be surprised by an unexpected question. Having answers ready will help show your child how to handle these situations as she takes over the responsibility and decides when and what to tell people about her adoption. When she chooses to open this door, she will inevitably find that she will be in the position of fielding such questions.

Transracial Adoption

Many people will not understand your desire to adopt transracially, and you may experience unexpected prejudices. Even those you know and love may surprise you. You will be asked many personal questions that may be inappropriate. You may also experience rude stares or unnecessary comments from strangers.

People may ask you if this is your child or may assume that you are babysitting or that your spouse is of the same race as your child. You will also get ridiculous questions such as will your child speak his native language (even if he is an infant who cannot talk) or is he a member of the Communist party.

Families who adopt transracially may find that they receive criticism within their own community and from those who are native to their child's birth country. Sometimes, friends or relatives who were less than thrilled at the prospect of your adoption may be even more standoffish once you are home. However, this type of attitude will quickly separate the women from the girls.

Post-Adoption Networking

Finding others who have been in or are standing in your shoes can be beneficial to adoptive families regardless of where they are in the process. As you move from pre-adoption to post-adoption, you will feel a sense of accomplishment and wish to serve as a mentor. In all likelihood, you have either met such a person or would like to have found one.

Oftentimes, new parents may have questions that in all likelihood have already been asked or experienced by other adoptive families. These topics could include child development, early education, attachment, paperwork, or medical concerns.

Many adoption agencies have Parents in Progress groups and offer a variety of post-adoptive family events, summer camps, or other services for their clients. If you are not using a local agency, consider contacting your local Council on Adoptable Children; they may be able to give you a recommendation.

You may find that there are non-agency-affiliated adoption support groups or playgroups in your area. You may also find a large spectrum of adoption support and advocacy organizations on the Internet. Some may be country-specific while others may be open to all adoptive families living within a geographical region.

You may also wish to consider a support organization so your child can meet and interact with other adopted children. Children who experience support from adopted peers may have a better understanding or appreciation of adoption. While we may take this for granted now, it may be more important as your child grows and matures.

Embassy Registration, Visitation, and Post-Placement

During the adoption process, you may have been asked to sign an agreement that you will register your child at their birth country's consulate or embassy in the United States. This is because your child will have dual citizenship until his or her eighteenth birthday. Even though the U.S. Government does not recognize it, your child is still considered a citizen of his or her birth country.

A few countries, including Moldova and, most recently, the St. Petersburg region of Russia, are asking families to sign consent forms allowing adoption officials from your child's birth country to visit your child. Part of the adoption fee in Moldova pays for the cost of this trip and a representative of the Moldavian Adoption Committee does visit adoptive families. It remains to be seen if this will actually happen to families who adopt from St. Petersburg.

While this may sound a bit intrusive, I do not believe there's a better way to promote adoption than letting the officials see for themselves how much our children have grown and flourished.

Most countries require regular post-placement reports after the completion of an adoption. When these reports are due and at what intervals will vary. Most adoption agencies wish to fulfill this obligation and will contact the family when post-placements are due.

For our second international adoption, we were required to sign a contract from the facilitating agency stating that if our adoption agency failed to provide adequate post-placements they had the right to assign an agency of their choice to ensure that these procedures were followed. We had no problem with this contract because we basically had already done this for Callie's post-placement reports.

If you had a less-than-ideal adoption process and have discontinued the relationship with your agency, you may have to be creative to fulfill this obligation. It may be necessary to schedule post-placements and deal directly with your social worker, a facilitator, the orphanage director at the Russian Consulate, or other adoptive families. It is imperative that adoptive parents comply with the terms of adoption and take responsibility for the completion of these reports.

Failure to complete post-placement reports ultimately results in more regulations and more difficulty in the completion of adoptions for other families who follow in your footsteps. Failing to provide post-placements may also help perpetuate unfounded rumors involving the treatment of adopted children. This can and does result in investigations and the suspension of adoptions.

Staying in Contact

Besides completing post-placement reports, we regularly send updates about Callie to the orphanage director and various members of our staff. If you are as fortunate as we were to have had an excellent facilitating staff during your adoption travel, you may wish to remain in contact with them.

You should get any addresses or phone numbers while you are with them. Many times adoption agencies will not release this information. I cannot think of a better legacy for your child than establishing a permanent relationship with those who helped you with your adoption.

Epilogue

Adoption is a great lesson in patience and faith. Like childbirth, it is a life-changing experience. It can, however, be completely life altering in ways that you may never expect. I have come to realize that my infertility is perhaps my greatest gift. It is responsible for countless blessings including a renewal of my faith. I have a firm belief that whatever child is supposed to be mine will be, but without faith to sustain me during the tough times I would have been lost.

That's not to say that our adoption journey has been easy. It hasn't been. I could not have done it without the support of my friends and family, especially Kathy and Merry, who (unfortunately for them) got to hear every complaint, whine, and moan. For example, during the infertility treatments, I had more than 300 injections, most of which were administered by my poor husband. Then the shots triggered changes and surges in my hormones and weight gains. Our quest to create a family has vastly expanded my horizons not to mention my dress size.

Our adoption journey has been a long and winding path. It includes the heartbreaking loss of our first Russian referral, a failed domestic adoption due to domestic adoption fraud, (the birth mother was convicted on Felony Grand Theft by Deception) choosing to adopt from Moldova only to have a moratorium issued on international adoptions just weeks after, trying to locate a child who was in the orphanage with our daughter and finally being unable to adopt from the same city that she was born.

But of course there is our daughter who made it all worth while. No words can describe the overwhelming joy the first time you see your child, the first smile, or the first time she says Mommy. These along with the first spontaneous, hug, kiss, or gift have the power to heal the memories of years of infertility, the loss of a child or numerous, sleepless nights waiting for your child.

When we adopted Callie, we did not feel that we had just adopted a child but that we had also adopted a city and a country as our own. We left Russia with a greater appreciation of how fortunate we are to have the many freedoms that we so often take for granted. Mother Russia has given us the most extraordinary gift of a child. In doing so, she granted us an opportunity to bear witness to the living conditions of millions of children around the world.

To have a working understanding of the economic and social factors that have led to the breakdown of the family which has produced countless children whose families can not afford to feed, clothe, or provide medical care is a burden that can only result in one taking action. These actions could include increasing adoption awareness, the creation of true "not for profit" adoption agencies, legislation to help protect families and make adoption more affordable, or helping children's aid organizations for countries where adoption is not recognized or is illegal.

Sincerely,
Denise Harris Hoppenhauer

Resources

Adoption Resources

Adopting.com
Information resource for prospective parent information and parenting
information
www.adopting.com

AdoptingFromRussia.com
Provides information for families who are adopting from Russia
www.adoptingfromrussia.com

Adoption.com
Great resource for all types of adoption information
www.adoption.com

The Adoption Guide
Consumer protection and advocacy for adopting families
www.theadoptionguide.com

Adoption Today
Bimonthly magazine about adoption
www.adoptinfo.net
(888) 924-6736

Adoption Travel.com
Resources for international adoption travel planning
www.adoptiontravel.com

Adoptive Families magazine
Bimonthly adoptive parent magazine; publishers of the annual *Adoption Guide*
www.AdoptiveFamiliesMagazine.com
(646) 366-0830

American Academy of Adoption Attorneys
Attorneys specializing in adoption and adoption-related laws
Box 33053
Washington, D.C. 20033
(202) 832-2222
www.adoptionattorneys.org

The American Adoption Congress (AAC)
Provides help with all areas of adoption
P.O. Box 42730
Washington, D.C. 20015
(202) 483-3399

Amrex Inc.
Adoption, Management, Resource-Expertise
www.amrex.org

Attach-China
Provides attachment information on children adopted from China
www.attach-china.org

Children Awaiting Parents
U.S. children waiting to be adopted
555 Blossom Rd., Suite 306
Rochester, NY 14610
(888) 835-8802
www.capbook.org

Comeunity
Provides adoptive resources including book reviews, medical and health information, special-needs adoption, and more
www.comeunity.com

Eastern European Adoption Coalition
A multifaceted adoptive family support organization; provides adoption information including agency references, travel, research, and more; lists groups for many Eastern European countries including Russia, also for single-parent, special-needs, older-child, baby and toddler adoptions, and Wee-care (FAE/FAS)
www.eeadopt.net/site/eeac/

The Evan B. Donaldson Adoption Institute
Nonprofit organization whose mission is to improve adoption; home of the "Adoption Institute Newsletter"
(212) 269-5080
www.adoptioninstitute.org

Families for Russian and Ukrainian Adoption (FRUA)
National association with local chapters
P.O. Box 2944
Merrifield, VA 22116
(703) 560-6184
www.frua.org

Families with Chinese Children (FCC)
Organization of families who have adopted from China
www.fwcc.org

Jewish Adoptive Families-Stars of David
Adoption information and support network
www.starsofdavid.org

Joint Council on International Children's Services
Affiliation of inter-country adoption agencies; promotes ethical practice and child welfare services
www.jcics.org

Journey Home Adoption Services
Assists with adoption preparation and provides educational resources
www.journeyhomeinc.com

Korean Adoption
www.adoptkorea.com

National Adoption Center
Provides referrals and information about special-needs adoption; photo listing of children legally free to adopt
1500 Walnut St., Suite 701
Philadelphia, PA 19102
(800) TO ADOPT
www.adopt.org

National Adoption Information Clearinghouse
Comprehensive resource on all aspects of adoption
330 C St. SW

Washington D.C., 20447
(703) 352-3488
www.calib.com/naic

National Council for Single Adoptive Parents
P.O. Box 55
Wharton, NJ 07885
www.adopting.org/ncsap.html

National Father's Network
For fathers of children with special needs
www.fathersnetwork.org

National Resource Center for Special Needs Adoption
16250 Northland Dr., #120
Southfield, MI 48075
(248) 443-7080

North American Council on Adoptable Children
Advocates for waiting children, adoption support groups, and subsidies
970 Raymond Avenue, Suite 106
St. Paul, MN 55114-1149
(615) 644-3036
www.nacac.org

Older Child Adoption On-line Magazine
For older-child adoptive families or those who are adopting an older
child; practical insights into older child adoption
www.olderchildadoption.com

OrphanDoctor.com
Adoption and medical resources for internationally adopted children, including medical research and definitions
www.orphandoctor.com

Pact
Support and placement services for children of color
www.pactadopt.org

Parent Network for the Post-Institutionalized Child
For parents of children who are adopted internationally
P.O. Box 613
Meadowlands, PA 15347
www.pnpic.org

Rainbow Kids International
International adoption publication
www.rainbowkids.com

Resolve
Infertility support, local chapter information
www.resolve.org

Russian Adoption.org
Resource for adoption from Russia and Russian adoption medical services
www.russianadoption.org

Sibling Information Network
Helps siblings of adopted children and adults
249 Glenbrook Rd., Suite U 64
Storrs, CT 06269
(203) 344-7500

Single Parent Resource Center
www.singleparentusa.com

Special Needs Adoptive Parents (SNAP)
409 Granville St., Suite 1150
Vancouver, British Columbia V6C 1T2
(604) 687-3114

Stars of David Int'l, Inc.
Information and support network for Jewish adoptive families
www.starsofdavid.org

4adopting.com
Host of the *Adoption Journal*
www.4adopting.com

Child Advocacy, State and Federal Agencies

Bureau of Citizenship and Immigration Services (BCIS)
www.bcis.gov/graphics/index.htm

Centers for Disease Control
Provides information on vaccinations and safe food and water when traveling
www.cdc.gov

Children's Defense Fund
Legal work, advocacy, education for children
www.childrensdefense.org

Hague Adoption Standards Project
Draft standards to accredit agencies that provide international adoption services per guidelines to implement the Hague Treaty on Intercountry Adoption
www.hagueregs.org

National Clearinghouse on Child Abuse and Neglect
Provides information on family violence.
(800) 394-3366

U.S. State Department Office of Children's Issues
Official information on international adoption law and BCIS requirements
www.travel.state.gov/adopt

U.S. Department of State
U.S. embassies and other diplomatic missions
www.usembassy.state.gov/

Physicians

Dr. Jane Aronson
International Pediatric Health Services, PLLC
151 East 62nd St., Suite 1A
New York, NY 10021
(212) 207-6666
Fax (212) 207-6665
www.orphandoctor.com
E-mail orphandoctor@aol.com

Dr. Eric Downing, M.D.
Available for consultations in Russia
www.russianadoption.org

Dr. Boris Gindis
The Boris Gindis Center/Center for Cognitive-Developmental Assessment
and Remediation
13 South Van Dyke Avenue
Suffern, NY 10901
(845) 357-2512
www.bgcenter.com

Dr Jerri Ann Jenista, M.D.
551 Second St.
Ann Arbor, MI 48103
(734) 668-0419
Fax (734) 668-9492
www.comeunity.com

Dr. Dana Johnson, M.D.
International Adoption Clinic
University of Minnesota
420 Delaware St. SE
Minneapolis, MN 55455
(612) 624-1164

Services and Support

Adoption Medical News
Information about adoption and health
www.adoptionmedicalnews.com

The American Academy of Allergy, Asthma, and Immunology
611 E. Wells St.
Milwaukee, WI 53202
(800) 822-2762

American Academy of Pediatrics
Has provisional sections on adoption and foster care; includes medical
recommendations for adopted children
www.aap.org/sections/adoption

Center for Cognitive Developmental Assessment and Remediation
Cognitive, language, behavioral, and educational assessment for internationally adopted children; Dr. Boris Gindis
www.bgcenter.com

CHADD-Children and Adults with Attention Disorders
Nonprofit organization serving individuals with attention
deficit/hyperactivity disorder
www.chadd.org

Child Welfare League of America
440 First St. NW, Third Floor
Washington, D.C. 20001-2085
(202) 638-2592

Children Unlimited
Attachment, adoption and family preservation, respite, mediation, and
education
www.children-unlimited.org

Clearinghouse on Disability Information
Office of Special Education and Rehabilitative Services
Room 3132, Switzer Building

Washington, D.C. 20202-2524
(202) 334-8241

Institute for Attachment and Child Development
www.instituteforattachment.org

March of Dimes Birth Defects Foundation
Community Services Department
1275 Mamaroneck Avenue
White Plains, NY 10605
(914) 428-7100

National Association of Psychiatric Treatment Centers for Children
1025 Connecticut Ave. NW, Suite 1012
Washington, D.C. 20036
(202) 857-9735

National Center for Children and Youth with Disabilities (NCYD)
P.O. Box 1492
Washington, D.C. 20013
(800) 695-0285

Operation Smile
Craniofacial/cleft lip and palate
www.operationsmile.org

Sensory Integration Network
www.sinetwork.org

Wide Smiles
Cleft lip and palate resource
www.widesmiles.org

Help Lines

American Cleft Palate Foundation
(800) 242-5338

American Council of the Blind
(800) 424-8666

Attention Deficit Disorder Association (ADDA)
(800) 487-2282

American Heart Association
(800) 242-8721

American Speech/Language/Hearing Help Line
(800) 221-2438

Autism Society of America
(301) 565-0433

Cancer Information Service of the National Cancer Institute
(800) 4-CANCER

The Celiac Spur Association
(402) 558-0600

Cleft Palate Foundation
www.cleft.com

Cystic Fibrosis Foundation
(800) FIGHT-CF

National Aids Hotline
(800) 342-2437

National Aids Information Clearinghouse
(800) 458-5231

National Alliance of Genetic Support Groups
(800) 336-4363

National Association for Perinatal Addiction Research and Education
(800) 638-2229

National Cerebral Palsy Association
(800) 872-5827

National Down Syndrome Congress
(800) 232-6372

National Institute of Neurological Disorders
(800) 352-9424

National Mental Health Association
(800) 969-6642

National Organization on Fetal Alcohol Syndrome
(202) 758-4585

United Cerebral Palsy Association
www.ucpa.org

Adoption Books

Adopting the Hurt Child: Hope for Families with Special-Needs Kids
Gregory C. Keck, Ph.D., and Regina M. Kupecky, LSW
Pinon Press, 1995 (Revised and Expanded, 1998)

Adopting the Older Child
Claudia L. Jewett
Harvard Common Press, 1978

The Adoption Resource Book
Lois Gilman
Perennial Library, 1987

Attaching in Adoption: Practical Tools for Today's Parent
Deborah D. Gray
Perspectives Press, 2001

The Broken Cord
Michael Dorris
Harper & Row Publishers, 1989

The Chinese Adoption Handbook: How to Adopt from China and Korea
John H. Maclean
Writers Club Press, 2003

The Complete Adoption Book
Laura Beauvais-Godwin and Raymond Godwin
Adams Media Corporation, 1997

Give Them Roots, Then Let Them Fly: Understanding Attachment Therapy
The Attachment Center at Evergreen, Inc., 1995

To order:
Attachment Center at Evergreen:
PO Box 2764
Evergreen, CO 80437-2764
(303) 674-1910

Holding Time
Martha G. Welch, MD
Simon & Schuster, 1988

Keys to Parenting an Adopted Child
Kathy Lancaster
Barron's Educational Services, Inc., 1996

Parenting with Love and Logic
Foster Cline, M.D. and Jim Fay
Pinon Press, 1990

The Primal Wound: Understanding the Adopted Child
Nancy Verrier
Gateway Press, Inc., 1993

Raising Adopted Children
Lois Ruskai Melina
HarperCollins, 1998

The Russian Adoption Handbook: How to Adopt a Child from Russia, Ukraine and Kazakhstan,
John H. Maclean
Writers Club Press, 2000

The Russian Word for Snow
Janis Cooke Newman
St. Martin's Press, 2001

Toddler Adoption: The Weaver's Craft
Mary Hopkins-Best
Perspectives Press, 1997

Twenty Things Adopted Kids Wish Their Adoptive Parents Knew
Sherrie Eldridge
Random House, 1999

With Eyes Wide Open: A Workbook for Parents Adopting International Children over Age One.
Margie Miller and Nancy Ward
LN Press, Incorporated, 1996

Where to Find Adoption Books

Perspectives Press
Publishes books on infertility and adoption
www.PerspectivesPress.com

Tapestry Books
Mail-order catalog with books on adoption and parenting issues
www.tapestrybooks.com

Other Books

The American Academy of Pediatrics, The Complete and Authoritative Guide, Caring for Your Baby and Young Child, Birth to Age 5

Steven P. Shelov, MD, F.A.A.P., Editor-in-Chief
Bantam Books, 1998

The Baby Book, Everything You Need to Know about Your Baby-from Birth to Age Two.
William Sears, M.D. and Martha Sears, R.N.
Little Brown and Company, 1993

Child of My Heart: A Celebration of Adoption
Barbara Alpert
Berkley Books, 1999

The Girlfriends Guide to Toddlers
Vickie Iovine
Penguin Putnam, 1999

The Pink and Blue Toddler and Preschooler Pages, Practical Tips and Advice for Parents
Laurie Waldstein and Leslie Zinberg
Contemporary Books, 1999

What to Expect, the Toddler Years
Arlene Eisenberg, Heidi E. Murkoff, and Sandee E. Hathaway, B.S. N.
Workman Publishing, 1996

Showers, the Complete Guide to Hosting a Perfect Bridal or Baby Shower
Beverly Clark
Wilshire Publications, 1989

Language and Travel Resources

Adopting from Russia, A Language and Parenting Guide
Adopting from China
Adopting from Latin America
By Teresa Kelleher
Tender Loving Communications
P.O. Box 90
Taylor, AZ 85939-0090
http://worknotes.com/AZ/AdoptingFromRussia/Kelleher/

Berlitz Essential Spanish
Berlitz Publishing Company, Inc., 1992

Berlitz Passport to 31 Languages (CD-ROM)
Includes Chinese, Korean, Romanian, Russian, Spanish, Vietnamese, and more.
The Learning Company, Inc.
www.learningco.com

Russia, Ukraine, and Belarus: A Lonely Planet Travel Survival Kit
John Noble, Andrew Humphreys, Richard Nebesky, Nick Selby, George Wesly, and John King
Lonely Planet Publications, 1996

Adoption-Related and Multicultural Gifts

A Mother's Charm
www.motherscharm.com

AdoptShoppe.com
Unique adoption gifts
www.adoptshoppe.com

AdoptionShop.com
www.adoptionshop.com

Asia for Kids
Language and culture resource; large selection of books, includes
China, Vietnam, Korea, India, Russia, and more
www.asiaforkids.com

Celebrate the Child
Large selection of products from Russia, China, Korea, Lain America,
Vietnam, Cambodia, and more
www.celebratechild.com

China Sprout
Chinese cultural products and services
www.chinasprout.com

Kremlin Gifts
Gifts from Russia including lacquer arts and gifts
Kremlin Gifts
Box 2
Fairfield, ME 04937
(207) 649-7853
www.kremlingifts.com

Maria's Children
Sponsored art rehabilitation program for Russian orphans
Maria's Children International

4321 W. Highway 13
Savage, MN 55378
(952) 895-1603
www.mariaschildren.org

Sovietski
Unique Russian and Eastern European gifts and collectibles
PO Box 81347
San Diego, CA 92138-1347
www.sovietski.com

Miscellaneous Products

Children's Disability Bookshop Catalog
The Disability Bookshop
P.O. Box 129
Vancouver, WA 98666-0129
(360) 694-2462

Childcare Resources

The International Nanny Association
Provides a directory and listing for affiliated agencies
125 S. 4th St.
Norfolk, VA 68701
(402) 691-9628

National Association for Childcare Resource and Referral Agencies
Three hundred member agencies around the country
(507) 287-2220

National Association for the Education of Young Children
Provides information on child-care options
1509 16th St. NW
Washington, D.C. 20036-1826
(800) 424-2460

National Association for Family Child Care
Can provide a list of accredited child-care providers
(800) 359-3817

References

Chapter 1: What's in a Name?
Deborah McCurdy, *Choosing a Name for Your Foreign-Born Child, Report on Intercountry Adoption 2000,* International Concerns for Children.

Chapter 2: Baby Showers and Gift Registry
Beverly Clark, *Showers, the Complete Guide to Hosting a Perfect Bridal or Baby Shower, Shower for an Adopted Baby* (Carpenteria, CA: Wilshire Publications, 1989).

Chapter 3: While You Are Waiting
John H. Maclean, *Russian Adoption Handbook: How to Adopt a Child from Russia, Ukraine and Kazakhstan,* (Lincoln, NE: Writers Club Press, 2000).

Chapter 5: The Nursery
William Sears, M.D.& Martha Sears, R.N., *The Baby Book* (Boston: Little, Brown & Company, 1993).
"Baby Registry Must Haves," Babies R Us, The Baby Superstore.
Arlene Eisenberg, Heidi E. Murkoff, and Sandee E. Hathaway, B.S.N., *What to Expect the Toddler Years* (New York: Workman Publishing, 1994).
Lois Ruskai Melina, *Raising Adopted Children: Practical Reassuring Advice for Every Adoptive Parent* (New York: HarperCollins Publishers, Inc., 1998).
Mary Hopkins-Best, *Toddler Adoption: The Weaver's Craft* (Indianapolis, IN: Perspectives Press, 1997).

Chapter 6: The Toy Box
William Sears, M.D.& Martha Sears, R.N., *The Baby Book* (Boston: Little, Brown & Company, 1993).

Chapter 7: Child Safety
Steven P. Shelvov, M.D. and Robert E. Hannemann, M.D., *The American Academy of Pediatrics, Caring for Your Baby and Young Child— Birth to Age Five* (New York: Bantam Books, 1998).
"What You Should Know about Strollers, What You Should Know about Childproofing Your Home, What You Should Know about Baby Bath Time," *USA Baby,* May 14, 1999, *www.babysroom.com*
William Sears, M.D.& Martha Sears, R.N., *The Baby Book* (Boston: Little, Brown & Company, 1993).
Arlene Eisenberg, Heidi E. Murkoff, and Sandee E. Hathaway, B.S.N., *What to Expect the Toddler Years* (New York: Workman Publishing, 1994).

Chapter 8: A Safe Outdoors
Laurie Waldstein and Leslie Zinberg, *The Pink and Blue Toddler and Preschooler Pages—Practical Tips and Advice for Parents* (Lincolnwood, IL: Contemporary Books, 1999).
Arlene Eisenberg, Heidi E. Murkoff, and Sandee E. Hathaway, B.S.N., *What to Expect the Toddler Years* (New York: Workman Publishing, 1994).

Chapter 9: Mealtime Mania
Mary Hopkins-Best, *Toddler Adoption: The Weaver's Craft* (Indianapolis, IN: Perspectives Press, 1997).
Richard C. Theur, Ph.D., Infant Nutritionist and Vice President of Research and Development, Beech-Nut Nutrition Corporation, "Feeding Your Baby Right, Allergies, Microwaving, Water, Juices."
William Sears, M.D.& Martha Sears, R.N., *The Baby Book* (Boston: Little, Brown & Company, 1993).

John H. Maclean, *Russian Adoption Handbook: How to Adopt a Child from Russia, Ukraine and Kazakhstan,* (Lincoln, NE: Writers Club Press, 2000).
Toddler, Crawler, and Sitter Product, June 30, 1999, www.gerber.com

Chapter 11: Diaper Care and Potty Training
William Sears, M.D.& Martha Sears, R.N., *The Baby Book* (Boston: Little, Brown & Company, 1993).
Steven P. Shelvov, M.D. and Robert E. Hannemann, M.D., *The American Academy of Pediatrics, Caring for Your Baby and Young Child—Birth to Age Five* (New York: Bantam Books, 1998).

Chapter 12: The Medicine Cabinet
Arlene Eisenberg, Heidi E. Murkoff, and Sandee E. Hathaway, B.S.N., *What to Expect the Toddler Years* (New York: Workman Publishing, 1994).
Steven P. Shelvov, M.D. and Robert E. Hannemann, M.D., *The American Academy of Pediatrics, Caring for Your Baby and Young Child—Birth to Age Five* (New York: Bantam Books, 1998).

Chapter 13: The Pediatrician
Steven P. Shelvov, M.D. and Robert E. Hannemann, M.D., *The American Academy of Pediatrics, Caring for Your Baby and Young Child—Birth to Age Five* (New York: Bantam Books, 1998).
William Sears, M.D.& Martha Sears, R.N., *The Baby Book* (Boston: Little, Brown & Company, 1993).
Dr. Dana Johnson, M.D., Ph.D., "International Adoption: New Kids, New Challenges, Evaluation after Arrival, Screening Tests, Immunizations"
"Is Your Child Sick?" The Alliance for South Carolina's Children, Columbia, S.C.

Chapter 14: Medical Considerations for Adopted Children
William Sears, M.D.& Martha Sears, R.N., *The Baby Book* (Boston: Little, Brown & Company, 1993).

Lois Ruskai Melina, *Raising Adopted Children: Practical Reassuring Advice for Every Adoptive Parent* (New York: HarperCollins Publishers, Inc., 1998).

Lois Gilman, *The Adoption Resource Book*, 3rd ed. (New York: HarperCollins Publishers, 1992).

Mary Hopkins-Best, *Toddler Adoption: The Weaver's Craft* (Indianapolis, IN: Perspectives Press, 1997).

Chapter 15: Child-care, Preschool, and Babysitters
Steven P. Shelvov, M.D. and Robert E. Hannemann, M.D., *The American Academy of Pediatrics, Caring for Your Baby and Young Child—Birth to Age Five* (New York: Bantam Books, 1998).

Mary Hopkins-Best, *Toddler Adoption: The Weaver's Craft* (Indianapolis, IN: Perspectives Press, 1997).

William Sears, M.D.& Martha Sears, R.N., *The Baby Book* (Boston: Little, Brown & Company, 1993).

Laurie Waldstein and Leslie Zinberg, *The Pink and Blue Toddler and Preschooler Pages—Practical Tips and Advice for Parents* (Lincolnwood, IL: Contemporary Books, 1999).

"Baby Sitting Reminders," the American Academy of Pediatrics, Tip, The Injury Prevention Program, (1994).

Chapter 17: International Adoption
Laurie Waldstein and Leslie Zinberg, *The Pink and Blue Toddler and Preschooler Pages—Practical Tips and Advice for Parents* (Lincolnwood, IL: Contemporary Books, 1999).

Russia-Consular Information Sheet, January 19, 1999, www.travel.state.gov. Dr. Jane Aronson "Immunizations for Families Going Abroad for Inter-country Adoption," June 12, 2000, www.orphandoctor.com

"Travel and Vacations, Child Safety Seats on Airplanes, Choosing the Correct Child Safety Restraint for Air Travel, Tips for Flying with a Child," May 14, 1999, www.parenting-qa.com

John H. Maclean, *Russian Adoption Handbook: How to Adopt a Child from Russia, Ukraine and Kazakhstan,* (Lincoln, NE: Writers Club Press, 2000).

Chapter 18: Packing For Your Trip
Laurie Waldstein and Leslie Zinberg, *The Pink and Blue Toddler and Preschooler Pages—Practical Tips and Advice for Parents* (Lincolnwood, IL: Contemporary Books, 1999).
Eldon C. Romney, "Packing for Travel to Russia," Eastern European Adoption Coalition, July 6, 1999, www.eeadopt.com
Dr. Jane Aronson, "Preparation for Travel to Another Land," July 16, 2000, www.orphandoctor.com

Chapter 19: Clothing to Pack
"What to Wear on the Trip of a Lifetime," Travel Tips by Tree of Life Adoption Center, June 11, 1999, www.toladopt.org

Chapter 20: While You Are There
Laurie Waldstein and Leslie Zinberg, *The Pink and Blue Toddler and Preschooler Pages—Practical Tips and Advice for Parents* (Lincolnwood, IL: Contemporary Books, 1999).
"Gift Giving," Travel Tips by Tree of Life Adoption Center, June 11, 1999, www.toladopt.org

Chapter 21: Home Sweet Home
John H. Maclean, *Russian Adoption Handbook: How to Adopt a Child from Russia, Ukraine and Kazakhstan,* (Lincoln, NE: Writers Club Press, 2000).
Harriet McCarthy, "Post Adoption Depression, The Unacknowledged Hazard," PAD Survey, Eastern European Adoption Coalition, 2000.
June Bond, "Post-Adoption Depression Syndrome," *Roots and Wings* 6 no.4 (Spring 1995).

About the Author

Denise Harris Hoppenhauer is an adoptive parent and an advocate. She currently resides in Greenville, South Carolina, with her husband, Michael, and their two children.

She is the founder of the Greenville Adoption Playgroup, the Greenville Chapter Leader of the South Carolina Council on Adoptable Children (SC COAC), and the 2003 recipient of the Dave Thomas Advocate of the Year Award from the SC COAC.

Denise is a program coordinator for an International Adoption Agency. She has had numerous adoption-related articles published in a variety of publications. This is her first book.

Ms. Hoppenhauer can be reached at Bunny@theHopps.com

The author is donating 10 percent of her proceeds to Shoes for Orphan Souls. Since 1999, Shoes for Orphan Souls has sent over 700,000 pairs of new shoes to orphanages in the United States and more than twenty-six countries. www.shoesfororphansouls.org

978-0-595-29724-5
0-595-29724-2

Made in the USA
Lexington, KY
21 January 2012